Camping Pennsylvania

HELP US KEEP THIS GUIDE UP TO DATE

Every effort has been made by the author and editors to make this guide as accurate and useful as possible. However, many things can change after a guide is published—campgrounds open and close, grow and contract; regulations change; facilities come under new management, etc.

We would love to hear from you concerning your experiences with this guide and how you feel it could be improved and kept up to date. While we may not be able to respond to all comments and suggestions, we'll take them to heart and also make certain to share them with the author. Please send your comments and suggestions to the following address:

GPP
Reader Response/Editorial Department
PO Box 480
Guilford, CT 06437

Or you may e-mail us at: editorial@GlobePequot.com

Thanks for your input, and happy travels!

Camping
Pennsylvania

A Comprehensive Guide to Public Tent and RV Campgrounds

Second Edition

Bob Frye

FALCONGUIDES

GUILFORD, CONNECTICUT

FALCONGUIDES®

An imprint of The Rowman & Littlefield Publishing Group, Inc.
4501 Forbes Blvd., Ste. 200
Lanham, MD 20706
www.rowman.com
Falcon and FalconGuides are registered trademarks and Make Adventure Your Story is a trademark of The Rowman & Littlefield Publishing Group, Inc.

Distributed by NATIONAL BOOK NETWORK

Copyright © 2021 The Rowman & Littlefield Publishing Group, Inc.

Photos by Bob Frye
Maps by Melissa Baker

British Library Cataloguing in Publication Information available

Library of Congress Cataloging-in-Publication Data available

ISBN 978-1-4930-5641-5 (paperback)
ISBN 978-1-4930-5642-2 (e-book)

∞™ The paper used in this publication meets the minimum requirements of American National Standard for Information Sciences—Permanence of Paper for Printed Library Materials, ANSI/NISO Z39.48-1992.

The author and The Rowman & Littlefield Publishing Group, Inc. assume no liability for accidents happening to, or injuries sustained by, readers who engage in the activities described in this book.

To all those who keep our natural places wild

Pennsylvania's public campgrounds serve as great base camps from which to explore the state. The viaduct in Kinzua Bridge State Park is not to be missed. Visitors can walk out on the old railroad platform, which stands 301 feet above the valley floor, and look down through a glass floor to the ground below.

Contents

Acknowledgments xi
Introduction 1
How to Use This Guide 4
Other "Camping" 11
Travel Tips 20
Camping with Kids 31
Tourism Information and Things to See and Do 33
Map Legend 34

Western Pennsylvania 35
1 Pymatuning State Park 39
2 Colonel Crawford Park 39
3 Two Mile Run County Park 40
4 Shenango River Lake 41
5 Mahoning Creek Lake–Milton Loop Campground 43
6 Crooked Creek Lake 43
7 Loyalhanna Lake 45
8 Keystone State Park 46
9 Raccoon Creek State Park 47
10 Ryerson Station State Park 48
11 Youghiogheny River Lake Outflow Campground 49
12 Youghiogheny River Lake Yough Lake Campground 50
13 Ohiopyle State Park 51
14 Kooser State Park 52
15 Laurel Hill State Park 53

Northern Pennsylvania 56
16 Willow Bay Recreation Area 61
17 Hooks Brook Boat Access Campground 62
18 Handsome Lake Boat Access Campground 63
19 Hopewell Boat Access Campground 63
20 Pine Grove Boat Access Campground 64
21 Dewdrop Recreation Area 65
22 Morrison Boat Access Campground 66
23 Kiasutha Recreation Area 67
24 Red Bridge Recreation Area 68
25 Buckaloons Recreation Area 69
26 Hearts Content Recreation Area 70
27 Minister Creek Campground 71
28 Chapman State Park 72
29 Tionesta Lake Outflow Recreation Area 73

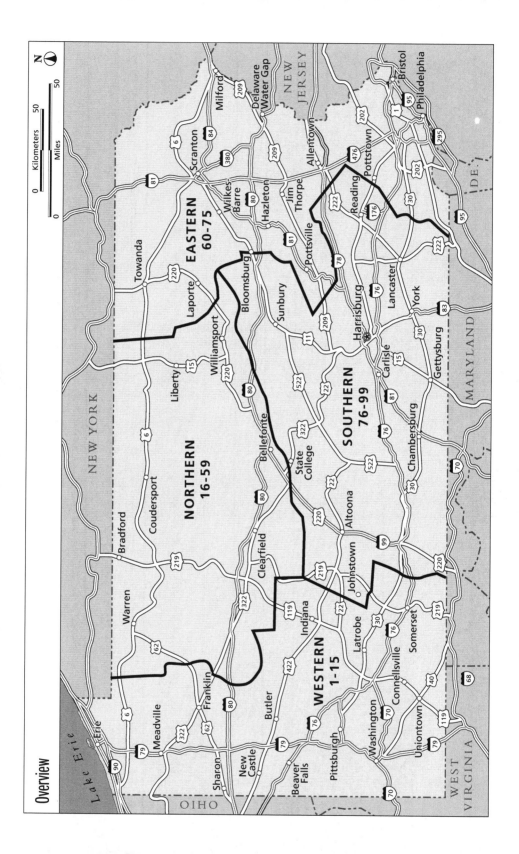

Overview

30 Tionesta Lake Recreation Area 74
31 Tionesta Lake Lackey Flats Camping Area 76
32 Tionesta Lake Glasner Run Camping Area 76
33 Tionesta Lake Kellettville Recreation Area.. 77
34 Loleta Recreation Area... 77
35 Cook Forest State Park 78
36 Clear Creek State Park 80
37 Twin Lakes Recreation Area 81
38 Tracy Ridge Recreation Area 82
39 Elk State Park 83
40 Parker Dam State Park 83
41 Simon B. Elliott State Park 85
42 Curwensville Lake 86
43 Black Moshannon State Park.. 86
44 Bald Eagle State Park 88
45 Ravensburg State Park 90
46 Little Pine State Park... 91
47 Hyner Run State Park 91
48 Kettle Creek State Park.. 92
49 Sinnemahoning State Park 93
50 Ole Bull State Park 94
51 Leonard Harrison State Park 95
52 Colton Point State Park 96
53 Lyman Run State Park.. 98
54 Cherry Springs State Park.. 99
55 Patterson State Park 99
56 Sizerville State Park... 100
57 Hills Creek State Park.. 101
58 Tioga–Hammond Lakes Ives Run Campground... 102
59 Cowanesque Lake Tompkins Campground.. 102

Eastern Pennsylvania 104
60 Hibernia County Park 108
61 Green Lane Park.. 108
62 Tohickon Valley Park 110
63 Lake Towhee Park.. 111
64 Tinicum Park... 112
65 Locust Lake State Park 113
66 Mauch Chunk Lake Park 114
67 Hickory Run State Park.. 115
68 Tobyhanna State Park 117
69 Promised Land State Park.. 118
70 Frances Slocum State Park.. 119
71 Lackawanna State Park 120

72 Ricketts Glen State Park 121
73 Worlds End State Park.. 123
74 Larnard–Hornbrook County Park 124
75 Sunfish Pond County Park.. 124

Southern Pennsylvania 127
76 Duman Lake County Park 131
77 Prince Gallitzin State Park.. 132
78 Blue Knob State Park.. 133
79 Trough Creek State Park 135
80 Raystown Lake Susquehannock Campground 137
81 Raystown Lake Seven Points Campground.............................. 137
82 Raystown Lake Nancy's Campground...................................... 138
83 Shawnee State Park... 140
84 Cowans Gap State Park... 141
85 Caledonia State Park... 142
86 Pine Grove Furnace State Park.. 143
87 Fowlers Hollow State Park 144
88 Colonel Denning State Park.. 145
89 Little Buffalo State Park 146
90 Penn–Roosevelt State Park.. 146
91 Greenwood Furnace State Park 147
92 Reeds Gap State Park.. 149
93 Poe Valley State Park 149
94 Poe Paddy State Park 150
95 Raymond B. Winter State Park.. 151
96 Gifford Pinchot State Park 153
97 Codorus State Park 153
98 Lancaster County Central Park.. 154
99 French Creek State Park 156

Appendix: Packing List 158
Campsite Index 162
About the Author 164

Acknowledgments

Pennsylvania is blessed with an abundance of public land, which means we've got lots of public campgrounds too. Some are small, meant generally for tents, in parks no bigger than the average family farm. Others are large, built with an engineer's eye for maximizing space, and located within parks that cover thousands or tens of thousands of acres or are surrounded by hundreds of thousands of acres of state or national forest.

The one thing they have in common is that they're run by dedicated managers, rangers, maintenance crews, and others who do a good job of providing fun places to be, all on generally too-small budgets. All of those I talked with were friendly, patient, and helpful. A thank-you to everyone.

Of course no book like this gets done without lots of help on the home front, so thanks to my wife, Mandy, and sons, Derek and Tyler, who, when they're not with me, keep things rolling along. Thank you for picking up the slack.

State park campgrounds account for more than half the public campgrounds in Pennsylvania.
Many, like Keystone State Park, are home to "campground hosts" who help newcomers settle in.

Introduction

Pennsylvania is a state that can take you by surprise.

Located in the Northeast and one of the thirteen original colonies, it's sometimes seen as small, smoky and industrial, packed and populous, tamed and long since wrangled. But that's not completely so. It's true that Pennsylvania is just the thirty-third largest state in America—about nine times as big as Connecticut but only about one-sixth the size of Texas and one-fourteenth the size of Alaska. Twelve million people live within its 46,000-plus square miles. And in Philadelphia and Pittsburgh it's got two cities big enough to host a combined seven professional sports teams. Philadelphia in particular is huge and dense, the fifth most heavily populated city in the nation.

Yet—and this is the amazing part—Pennsylvania has a generous amount of open space, much of it publicly owned, that's stunningly beautiful. Breaking the state into northern, southern, eastern, and western regions, this book reveals opportunities to explore all kinds of wild country and experience all varieties of camping in all sorts of settings.

The northern part of the state, the so-called Pennsylvania Wilds in the eyes of state tourism officials, is within a day's drive of more than half the nation and only 10 hours from Chicago. Yet the area is home to millions of acres of woodlands—the largest block of public land between New York and the Windy City. It's so remote that in some counties, hunting camps and cottages outnumber full-time, year-round residences, and the total number of traffic lights can be counted on one finger. In a state rich with wildlife, this is where you'll have the greatest chance to encounter species from black bears and bobcats to otters and porcupines. It's not all wilderness though. There are some unique and interesting communities to be found here. But overall this is the place to go if you like to camp in a world where the typical "town" has one—maybe—four-pump gas station and you shop for bait, motor oil, shampoo, and bread all in the same tiny store.

Western Pennsylvania is different. It offers everything from mountains—including Mount Davis, the highest point in the state at 3,213 feet—and rolling, steep-sided hills in the south to wetlands and lakes in the north. Variety is the buzzword. But its attractions are in general closer to the "beaten path." If that means you won't always feel lost here—even if you can find some pretty wild places if you look—you can at least count on being able to get from one attraction to the next. For example, you can fish Lake Erie in the morning, drive down I-79 in the afternoon and catch a Pittsburgh Pirates ball game, then follow the Pennsylvania Turnpike or the Lincoln Highway east to spend the night in a tent in the wooded mountains of the Laurel Highlands. Travel a little slower and you can fish, hike, and paddle and visit museums, shopping malls, and fairs. There's simply a lot to see and do, all of it easily accessible from interstates and other highways.

The state's southern quarter is the breadbasket of sorts, where large agriculture is king. There are some state forests and a lot of state parks, to be sure. This is where the state's first forestry school was established and its first foresters trained, so there's a tradition tied to all those woods. There's water to boat on and fish to catch. And there's plenty of history as well. Gettysburg, site of the iconic Civil War battle, is nearby. But don't forget all the good food available. Roadside farm stands selling everything from apple butter and cider to sweet corn, peaches, and cherries will greet you everywhere you go.

And the east? This is people country. The southernmost part of the region, around Philadelphia, is the most intensely populated part of the state by far. Open space is at a premium, as is solitude. But don't let that fool you. There's a surprising amount of wildlife to be found here and some very interesting places in which to see it. Meanwhile, if you drive north toward the Poconos, the amount of open space increases. It's not as remote as the Wilds—the region's proximity to New York City, less than a three-hour drive away, makes it a playground for lots and lots of people—but you can still find lots of room to do your thing, whether that be to partake of some of the best whitewater rafting anywhere or to fish on a large lake or even some tidal waters.

Taken together, across all those miles, the state offers the chance to encounter varied and charismatic wildlife. Some of the largest black bears in the world—animals that can top 800 pounds, more than the typical Lower 48 grizzly—live within the state's borders, growing fat on everything from acorns and berries to fawns, mice, and bugs. Bald eagles, once all but vanished, have returned, as have peregrine falcons, the world's fastest bird of prey. There are bobcats, otters, and fishers, a large member of the weasel family. There are elk, white-tailed deer, geese, ducks, herons, brook trout, largemouth and smallmouth bass, 50-inch class muskies, and more.

As a camper you can most typically encounter all that wildlife across three seasons. Although a few public campgrounds are open year-round, most operate from spring through late to early fall. Many tie their opening to the first day of the state's trout fishing season, which falls in mid-April across most of the state, and their closing to Labor Day, the peak of the colorful foliage season in mid-October, or the state's firearms deer hunting season, which falls in the first two weeks of December. Virtually all campgrounds allow you to stay a minimum of fourteen consecutive days, so you have time to relax and get settled.

The weather across those seasons can vary widely, depending on where you are. Generally the portion of Pennsylvania north of I-80 gets cold in the fall first, hangs on to winter longest, and warms up last in the spring. The area around Lake Erie can be exceptionally hairy. It sometimes gets "lake effect" storms that can generate giant waves if you're on the water or bury you under lots of sudden snow onshore. The southeast corner of the state, meanwhile—close enough to the Delaware Bay and Atlantic Ocean that you have to worry about the tides if you paddle at the John Heinz National Wildlife Refuge—warms up the quickest each year, one reason that trout fishing season opens earlier there than elsewhere.

Pennsylvania is home to a surprising variety of wildlife, including bobcats. Wildlife officials believe they are more numerous and widespread in the state today than since at least 1970.

Across all those months there are wonderful opportunities to hike and bike to waterfalls and overlooks, ride horses across meadows and through woods, paddle or motor down rivers and across lakes, explore history, and fish, hunt, play, and just relax.

Hopefully this book will help you explore some of the Keystone State's wild and wonderful country, spending the night here and there, while taking in the beauty of its woods, fields, fish, and wildlife. Enjoy!

How to Use This Guide

Overview

This is a comprehensive look at the public campgrounds in Pennsylvania: those run in state parks by the Department of Conservation and Natural Resources, in Allegheny National Forest by the USDA Forest Service, at lakes owned by the US Army Corps of Engineers, and by assorted counties. These are the places where you pull in, pay a fee—though not always—and set up shop at a designated, numbered site, with an expectation that there will be amenities of some sort. We tell you what to expect at each campground and what you can look forward to doing while you are there.

We also tell you, if in slightly less detail, about the other options when it comes to camping on public land in Pennsylvania. There's a lot of "dispersed" camping—the kind of thing where you create your own site—available in state and national forests, and we tell you how that works. There are also some designated backpacking areas that offer things like water and restrooms; we talk about those a bit too.

You can sometimes "camp" under a roof. In some Pennsylvania campgrounds you can rent cabins—some modern, with running water and showers; some log holdovers from the 1930s that are more like an old trapper's cabin. There are also cottages, yurts—if you don't know what those are, you will—and even some interesting old houses you can book. We describe those opportunities too.

Private campgrounds are not covered here. There are hundreds if not thousands of those spread around Pennsylvania. Many are the kind of place where people set up trailers and leave them year-round; others cater to weekend tent campers and the like. Details on many of these campgrounds are available from the Pennsylvania Campground Owners Association. For more information visit pacamping.com or call (610) 767-5026.

Types of Campgrounds

State Parks

Pennsylvania's Department of Conservation and Natural Resources administers Pennsylvania's state park system, which has been set up so that there is a park within 25 miles of every state resident. There are 121 state parks in all, 54 of them with campgrounds open to tents and RVs.

Some parks are big, covering thousands of acres. Others are smaller than 100 acres, though typically surrounded by much larger state forests. Many have lakes and/or streams. Some have playgrounds, and one has a golf course; others are pure woods.

The state's park system has been ranked one of the best in the country. In 2009 it was awarded the prestigious National Gold Medal Award for Excellence in Park and Recreation Management by the American Academy for Park and Recreation Administration and the National Recreation and Park Association. The medal is awarded only every two years and is akin to an actor winning an Academy Award, so it's big stuff.

The park system was honored for a number of reasons, including its emphasis on green practices, its conservation ethic, and its resource management. The parks were also recognized for something that will be more noticeable to campers: their "Get Outdoors PA" initiative. It's morphed over time, but gives park visitors all kinds of ideas on how to get outside and play. There are fact sheets, videos, webinars, and tips on how and where to take part in activities from archery shooting to backpacking to mountain biking and more. Details can be found at getoutdoorspa.org/.

Meanwhile, many parks offer in-person programs aimed at teaching people how to enjoy the outdoors. Visitors can learn how to go backpacking, birding, hiking, camping, cross-country skiing, fly-fishing, geocaching, horseback riding, mountain biking, orienteering, rock climbing, canoeing and kayaking, snowshoeing, and white-water rafting, as well as learn wilderness survival, outdoor ethics, and nature photography. Some programs are aimed specifically at children, others at adults and teenagers, but most are family-friendly so that the entire gang can take part. In all cases, trained environmental educators and experts in various endeavors serve as guides and often provide all the equipment needed on a loaner basis.

Programs are scheduled from spring through fall and are listed in an online calendar that you can view at events.dcnr.pa.gov. Visit it and you can tie your camping trip to a particular park or activity.

If you find a park you really enjoy, consider becoming a campground host. Most parks are always looking for one or more hosts, who "work" 40 hours a week in an unpaid volunteer position. The job largely involves being the go-to person for new campers who check in and have questions about things like campground rules, where to get firewood, and where to hike. Hosts stay at each park for free for a minimum of two weeks, sometimes longer. Check with your favorite park for program details.

USDA Forest Service

Pennsylvania is home to one national forest, the Allegheny, which covers more than 517,000 acres. The vast majority, about 463,000 acres, are forested, but there are also 42,000 acres of fields and meadows and 11,000 acres of water, most of that the Allegheny Reservoir, also known locally as Kinzua Dam. The park is divided into two ranger districts: Bradford and Marienville.

The forest service motto of "Land of Many Uses" applies here, for better and worse. The good is that there's plenty to do here if you like to be outside. There's quiet paddling as well as big, open water for skiing and tubing. There are tiny brook trout streams to fish as well as deep waters holding muskies, pike, and walleyes. There are plenty of woods to hunt—sportsmen migrate here from all over Pennsylvania each fall—and hike, all manner of wild creatures on the landscape, and trails to travel by horseback and on all-terrain vehicles. The bad is that there are only two officially designated wilderness areas on the Allegheny—8,600-acre Hickory Creek and 400-acre Allegheny Islands—so you won't cover mile upon mile without cutting a road, be it paved or dirt, somewhere.

Allegheny National Forest boasts a number of campgrounds. Here a pair of anglers walk past the entrance to the Minister Creek Campground to fish for brook trout.

But the forest doesn't feel too broken, especially in comparison with the rest of the state. And there are lots of options when it comes to camping. The forest is home to more than a dozen established campgrounds, some of them boat-in only, as well as dispersed sites, some of them officially recognized, others of the make-your-own-space variety. If you can't find something to suit your tastes here, you're not trying.

US Army Corps of Engineers

Corps-managed land in Pennsylvania is divided into three segments: the Pittsburgh, Baltimore, and Philadelphia districts. All serve the same primary purpose: to manage locks and dams on the state's rivers and to offer flood control via its impoundments. Providing recreation is a secondary part of the Corps' mission.

That said, Corps impoundments do offer plenty for those who love the outdoors. Lakes within the Pittsburgh and Baltimore districts are home to a dozen campgrounds. These are often open, sunny, no-frills sites. Picture rows of camping pads in a manicured field, albeit with electrical hookups and picnic tables, and you get the idea. There are exceptions though.

In all cases, water-based activities are the draw at Corps facilities. Many surround large bodies of water where boats can operate without horsepower restrictions and visitors can enjoy activities like powerboating, tubing, waterskiing, and the like. That makes these facilities unique in comparison to most state and county parks.

Corps-managed facilities do not offer as much as state parks in the way of programming, but you can do more than boat. You can also hike, go horseback riding, and hunt in season, for example.

County Campgrounds

Pennsylvania is divided into sixty-seven counties, and a surprising number of them offer public camping. With a couple of notable exceptions, county parks are generally smaller in overall size. Their campgrounds are correspondingly smaller and sometimes capable of handling only tents or shorter RVs. The camping season can be shorter too.

But several of these campgrounds are located in the southeastern corner of the state, where other public options are limited; this alone makes them valuable.

If you're the leader of a group, such as a Scout troop, your county options are greater. A number of county parks that do not allow public camping will make exceptions for organized groups and let you pitch tents, typically in a field or along a woodline. You'll find no campground facilities but will be able to get water and use restrooms open to day-use visitors. If you're interested in that kind of thing, it's worth making a call to the county parks or planning department and asking for permission.

Campground Entries

This book divides the state's campgrounds into four regions: Western, Northern, Eastern, and Southern Pennsylvania. For purposes of organizing state parks—which account for about half of all the public campgrounds in the state—the Department of Conservation and Natural Resources divides Pennsylvania the same way. You can see the listing at www.dcnr.pa.gov/Recreation/WhatToDo/StayOvernight/Pages/default.aspx.

Maps within this book give you an at-a-glance look at the campgrounds in each region. Charts detail the amenities and recreational opportunities they offer. There's also a short but specific overview of each region outlining its history, geography, and attractions.

Each campground also gets its own listing, including the following details:

Location: This is the nearest town that shows up on a map so that you can get your general bearings.

Season: This is the period when the campground is open. Here are a few things to keep in mind.

First, while all the parks mentioned in this book are open to visitors year-round, most of the campgrounds within them are two- or three-season operations. And

Visitors to Kettle Creek State Park will be wowed by the scenery of the Kettle Creek valley, shown here in all its glory just upstream of the park's Lower Campground.

within that window, facilities can sometimes vary. For example, a campground that offers flush toilets and showers in midsummer may operate only vault toilets in fall. It's always best to call the campground to be sure.

Second, you can expect larger-than-normal crowds on a couple of weekends specific to Pennsylvania. A lot of campgrounds list their opening as "mid-April." That's opening weekend of trout fishing season in three-quarters of the state. That Saturday in particular is the single busiest fishing day of the year, when more than 750,000 anglers will be on the water. Camp then and you'll likely have lots of fishermen as neighbors. Likewise, some campgrounds stay open to mid-December to accommodate hunters during the deer season that runs for two weeks starting the Saturday after Thanksgiving. There's no hunting allowed within campgrounds, but you may have more company than you'd expect for that late in the year.

Third, campgrounds periodically close for maintenance or other reasons, so always check in advance to be sure a campground will be open when you get there.

Sites: This tells you the total number of campsites available and a little bit about them. Some, for example, are walk-in only; others may have electricity or be ADA accessible. Increasing numbers in state parks offer full-service hookups.

Maximum RV length: How big an RV can the campground accommodate? You'll find that information here. State parks in particular now accommodate some larger RVs than before, but there are some that are limited to smaller ones, too.

Be aware, though, that not all the pads within a campground are equally long. A campground that says it can accommodate 75-foot RVs may have just one site that big, with the rest 50 feet or shorter. If you've got an especially large rig, call ahead to make sure you can get the space you need.

Facilities: Does the campground have flush toilets and showers or outhouses? Electricity and a sanitary dump station? How about a camp store or a launch for your boat? This section tells you what facilities are available at the campground.

Fee per night: Prices change constantly and can even vary within a campground based on whether you're taking a walk-in tent site, a boat-in site, or one with electric service for a 40-foot RV. Because of that, we've used a coded system.

$ = Less than $10

$$ = $10 to $15

$$$ = $16 to $20

$$$$ = More than $20

If the price code for a campground indicates a range (say, $–$$$), that means you've got options.

A few parks, as noted in the individual descriptions, offer cabins, cottages, and even lodges. We note their availability, but be aware that the price codes do not account for them. You'll need to call individual parks or check out the reservation systems for those fees.

Persons 62 years of age or older can receive a reduction on the base campsite fee at any campground operated by the Pennsylvania Bureau of State Parks. Allegheny National Forest likewise has discounted permits for seniors. Inquire about the discount through any forest service office.

Pets: Some campgrounds allow leashed pets in all their sites; others limit pets to certain sites, and some don't allow them at all.

Activities: Does the campground or surrounding area have hiking or mountain biking trails? A pool or a swimming beach? Does it offer environmental education programming or fishing and hunting opportunities? This section tells you what you can do in the campground and the park around it.

Management: This is the agency that owns and operates the campground.

Contact: Here you get the website for the park that holds this campground. Those websites often offer details on such things as the park's history, updates on conditions or changes, firewood availability or restrictions, other advisories, and more. You can sometimes find maps here too. That's especially true of state park websites, which offer maps of the park, campgrounds, and sometimes hiking or birding trails.

This section also offers the phone number for each park and/or campground. You'll note that some of the smallest state parks are all managed from one central office.

Also listed are details on whether campgrounds accept reservations—some do not—and how to make them. When it comes to federal and state campgrounds, you can make reservations online or by phone. County park campgrounds usually require that you make a phone call.

Of course you can take your chances on getting space on a walk-in basis just about anywhere, paying your fees on the honor system. But that can be risky at peak times. If you want to be sure there's a site waiting for you when you arrive at a park, call ahead.

Finding the campground: These are turn-by-turn directions to the campground and/or park from the nearest town that shows up on a map. The office is your best spot to pick up maps, brochures, and other information.

GPS coordinates: These coordinates were generated using mapping software. In most cases they will take you to the campground. In parks with more than one campground, the coordinates take you to the park office.

A word of caution here: Because of the remote character of the so-called "Wilds" of northern Pennsylvania, following a GPS device rather than using a map can take you over narrow, often rough, dirt forest service roads. In some instances these devices have directed users to follow "roads" that are in fact only power line or gas line rights-of-way. It's for that reason that many parks in this region did not, as of the time this book was published, encourage people to use GPS coordinates to find their way.

Other: If the campground or park offers cabins or cottages, hosts special events like a lumberjack or craft festival, or contains a theater, you'll find that information here. We also tell you if the park has an organized group tenting area, in case you want to camp here with scouts or some other group.

About the campground: Here you get a few tips on whether the campground is spacious or a bit cramped, which sites offer the best views or access to hiking or the water, whether sites are shaded or in the sun, and more.

Why it's worth a visit: Of all the campgrounds in the state, why make a point of visiting this particular one? That's what you'll learn here.

You can find space to take a walk just about anywhere, but some parks are renowned for their trails and the views they lead to. Many parks offer lakes. Some are open to boats with giant motors that can haul skiers; others are small and perfect for exploring on misty mornings with a canoe or kayak. You can expect to see squirrels and raccoons or at least evidence of them in every park you visit. But some are the gateways to viewing the state's herd of majestic elk.

The descriptions here explain what it is that makes each park, and each campground, special. They also tell you when might be the best time to visit. If you want to fish the famous hatches that come off some streams, you'll want to be there in May or June. If you want to hear bugling elk, you'll visit some places starting in September. If you want to hike through blazing orange, red, and yellow leaves, you'll visit during the peak of the fall foliage season in October.

Other "Camping"

If you've got a tent to pitch or an RV to park, there are other public options available to you in Pennsylvania than its "official" campgrounds. There is what's known as dispersed motorized camping, some backpacking that's managed by the state park system, and even shelters in a variety of shapes. We'll touch on each briefly.

Dispersed Camping

Pennsylvania's state forest system, run by the Department of Conservation and Natural Resources, is divided into twenty districts and comprises about 2.2 million acres. Its dispersed camping comes in a couple of forms.

First there's what's known as motorized camping. Under its guidelines you can park and set up camp just about anywhere in a state forest where you can find a wide spot in the road. A few districts, like Forbes and Sproul State Forests, have designated motorized sites. You won't find much there; a handful offer picnic tables and a fire ring, but they're the exception. All such sites can be reserved by calling the district forest office. Some are close to roads; others are located behind locked gates to which campers receive the keys or combinations. For these sites, campers are required to call the appropriate forest district office and get a permit. That usually involves a fee. If you try one of these, plan your outing in advance. Use of dispersed sites has been growing in popularity in recent years, so you can't count on a space being available on short notice. Permits can be secured ninety days in advance.

Across most of the rest of the state forest districts, campers just do their thing where they find a spot. This type of camping is particularly popular with anglers looking to get right on a trout stream, hunters interested in stomping around a particular valley, hikers looking to access a particular set of challenges, or all-terrain-vehicle riders looking to do their thing on some of the state forest system's nearly 250 miles of ATV trails. Some people pull over in motor homes as big as school buses; others pitch tents along the road's edge. In all such cases, a free permit is still required.

Visitors who camp this way need to provide their own water and have to account for their garbage and waste. There are some rules to follow too: For example, you have to park within 300 feet of the road, be at least 200 feet from a stream or water source, and stay 300 feet from natural areas. Some rules vary by forest district. In places, for example, campers are limited to two vehicles and ten people per site. You can find all the rules and a brochure at www.dcnr.pa.gov/Recreation/WhatToDo/StayOvernight/BackpackingAndPrimitiveCamping/Pages/default.aspx.

Finally, be aware that some forest roads are gravel and dirt and get no winter maintenance, so the spot that's perfect in summer may not be accessible later in the year.

Similar opportunities exist within Allegheny National Forest, though the rules are a bit confusing. Look at the forest's website—www.fs.usda.gov/allegheny—and it lists

Pennsylvania parks and forests are home to some "other" types of accommodations, such as this rustic 1930s-era cabin at Linn Run State Park.

a dozen dispersed camping areas. A few of those are more like actual campgrounds than anything else and are described in more detail later in this book. Other locations on the list do indeed talk about parking lots where you can spend the night. But forest officials actually discourage anyone from camping at many of those lots, which are trailheads. They don't want day users, hikers, backpackers, and others to have to walk through someone else's campsite to get on the trail.

A couple of onetime campgrounds have been turned into dispersed motorized sites on the Allegheny too. Bear Creek was shut down as an official campground years ago, so there are no designated sites, no facilities, and no amenities. But people still camp there. Likewise, Red Mill Pond camping area is just slightly more developed than the typical wide spot in the road—it's listed as a campground on the national forest website—but there are no official sites and no facilities here either.

All that said, there are wonderful opportunities to camp out on your own. Fans of ATVs make good use of these sites, setting up along the road near the national forest's 100 or so miles of ATV trails—80 of them in the Marienville District, 20 or so in the Bradford District—since there are no regular campgrounds near the trails. Equestrians also enjoy this option, especially on the 38-mile bridle trail system in the Duhring area of the Marienville District around what once was the Kelly Pines campground.

There are some rules to keep in mind: You can't camp within 1,500 feet of the shoreline at Allegheny Reservoir and features like Jakes Rock and Rimrock, and you can't camp within 1,500 feet of the road in other places. However, there's no fee to camp and no permits are required.

Dispersed, motorized camping is not for everyone. But this is a fun option if you're comfortable doing things on your own, don't need a lot in the way of amenities, and like quiet.

Backpacking

State forests and the Allegheny National Forest are both perfect spots for backpacking. You can do it without a lot of paperwork too. Permits are never a bad idea; that way someone knows where you are, when you're going in, and when you're expecting to come back out. But state forest rules don't require you to secure a permit as long as you don't plan to stay more than one night in any particular spot and won't be having a campfire. Keep moving, carry a stove, and you're free to roam as you please.

If you're new to backpacking and want to experience it without cutting ties completely, Oil Creek, Raccoon Creek, Laurel Ridge, and Moraine State Parks afford that opportunity. Each park has a backpacking trail that has "camps" along the way where you can pitch a tent you carry in or sleep in an Adirondack-style shelter that you rent. The sites typically offer water—though sometimes in limited quantities—and less occasionally even vault toilets. Some of the shelters are fronted with fireplaces and chimneys for cooking and heating; others are just lean-tos. All are walk-in only.

Oil Creek has the 36-mile Gerard Hiking Trail. It's a loop with two camp areas, but they're not spaced evenly, so this is either a two-day hike with lots of walking or a three-day hike featuring shorter legs. There's water here, toilets, even firewood provided by the park at times. You can rent sites eleven months in advance.

Raccoon Creek's loop backpacking trail is 19.5 miles long, also with sites at two spots along the way. This trail follows dirt and gravel roads at times and is the newest in the park system, so it doesn't yet get quite the use as some of the others. But it's a fun hike.

Moraine State Park is home to 13.9 miles of the 4,600-mile North Country National Scenic Trail. It's got one site, with one shelter. There's no special room for tents, no water, and no restrooms; this is a do-it-yourselfer all the way. But if you combine this with 12 connecting miles of trail in McConnells Mill State Park and Jennings Environmental Education Center—neither of which offers camping of any kind—this can be a good two-day, one-way trek.

The Laurel Highlands Hiking Trail, which runs through Laurel Ridge State Park as well as some other parklands, is the granddaddy of this kind of backpacking trail. It stretches 70 miles from end to end, running from Ohiopyle State Park in the south to the town of Seward in the north, traversing state park, forest, and game lands. Its middle section runs along ridgetops and is relatively flat, but its ends will test you. With its steep climbs and falls, the section from Ohiopyle to the first set of shelters in particular will reward you with spectacular scenery but bust your lungs along the way.

The trail features eight overnight sites, each with five shelters and room for tents, so you can do this trip over a week. There are fire rings, fireplaces, and pit toilets at each site, but water is iffy. You'll want to check with Laurel Ridge park officials about its availability before heading out.

To learn more about the four parks and their trails, visit www.dcnr.pa.gov/ Recreation/WhatToDo/StayOvernight/BackpackingAndPrimitiveCamping/Pages/ default.aspx

Cabins, Cottages, Yurts, and Unique Houses

Camping, by definition, involves staying in a tent, RV, or perhaps an Adirondack-style shelter. For most people, that is. For some, staying in a cabin or a cottage or something of the sort also qualifies. And Pennsylvania, primarily through its state park system, offers those kinds of opportunities.

One of the real benefits of this kind of "camping" is tied to the seasons. Many of these facilities remain open year-round, after campgrounds close, and so are popular with people looking for a place to stay while hunting, cross-country skiing, snow-shoeing, or just exploring the woods in winter. But people use them year-round for family gatherings or to stay with friends and family who can't or won't sleep in a tent.

These structures come in several forms: rustic and modern cabins, cottages, yurts, and even some unique dwellings.

Rustic Cabins

Rustic cabins date back to the 1930s or thereabouts. They typically sleep two to eight people in bunk and twin beds. Many were originally built by the men of the Civilian Conservation Corps (CCC) and they look the part—made of stone and logs, with fireplaces or woodstoves. Stay in one and you'll feel like you're at an old-time outpost. These cabins will require some work on your part though. Many are heated with gas, but only to the mid-50-degree range, so you'll need to burn firewood to stay warm in winter. They come with a stove, refrigerator, and microwave, and some have kitchen sinks with running water. None have indoor bathrooms. Renters get a key to the one centrally located shower house in each cabin cluster, which has indoor plumbing and sometimes laundry facilities, and can use the vault toilets nearby. But that's it. These are as minimalist facilities as cabins go.

Modern Cabins

Modern cabins are structures built within the past two decades that feature all the amenities of home. They have electric heat, bathrooms with showers and running water, a full kitchen, carpeting, and furniture beyond an indoor picnic table. Cathedral ceilings in the main living area and two to three bedrooms give them a capacity of up to eight people, making these homes away from home. They have no fireplaces, but fire rings outside allow making s'mores, mountain pies (sandwiches of toasted bread stuffed with pizza toppings or pie fillings cooked over the coals of a campfire), and other camping favorites. As with the rustic cabins, renters need to bring their own bedding and pillows, cooking equipment and utensils, and other camping gear. These are pricier than rustic cabins but not terribly so.

Both rustic and modern cabins must be rented for a week at a time, beginning on a Friday, but no longer, during peak season, which begins the second Friday in June and runs to the day before the third Friday in August. Throughout the rest of the year, cabins can be rented for a two-day minimum up to a maximum of fourteen consecutive days.

In years past dogs were not allowed in cabins. That's changed. The state park system now allows pets in some cabins around the state.

People can bring no more than two dogs to any one cabin, and the dogs or pets—and there are definitions of what qualifies—have to be licensed and current in their rabies vaccinations. They have to be free of ticks, fleas, worms, and mange. And they have to be friendly: Any dogs deemed aggressive have to go. Dog owners have to keep their pets under control at all times, have to be able to keep them from barking excessively, and can't leave them unattended in a cabin. Owners also have to certify that their dogs are house trained and are responsible for picking up any animal waste outside. Violating any of those rules is cause for being charged for damages and even being asked to take your dog home.

Information on camping with pets in state parks, whether in a cabin or a campground, can be found at www.dcnr.pa.gov/StateParks/RulesAndRegulations/Pets InParks/Pages/default.aspx.

Camping Cottages

These are a step down from cabins in terms of what they offer. They look cabin-like, with wooden walls and floors, windows, electric lights and outlets, and a porch. They'll sleep five people in single and double bunks. But they do not have kitchens or running water. And as with rustic cabins, bathrooms and showers will be located nearby but not within the cottage itself.

Instead these are places where you cook outside, as though you were tent camping or even picnicking, but where you sleep under a roof and in a bed at night. Sometimes these are located within a park's campground. Sometimes they're located outside a campground but nearby. Campers can stay for up to fourteen consecutive nights from Memorial Day to Labor Day and for up to twenty-one consecutive nights during the rest of the year.

Yurts

So what exactly is a yurt? That's the first thing most people ask about these funny-looking abodes.

Yurts, circular structures modeled after the portable houses of Asian nomads, are available for rent in several state parks.

Yurts are circular cottages, you might say, descended from similar structures used by nomads in Mongolia, Turkey, and other parts of the world centuries ago. With those yurts, the sides were animal skins, and the whole thing was made to be put up and taken down over and over as tribes moved around in search of food, much like the Plains Indians of the American West used tepees. Today's yurts feature sides and a top of heavy fabric. Inside, though, is where the real difference lies. They have kitchenettes with a stovetop, microwave, and refrigerator; single and double bunks capable of sleeping five people total; and a small table. Outside they often have picnic tables on a porch and fire ring nearby. These are the newest thing in state park camping, and they've spread from a few parks to more than a dozen statewide thus far.

Deluxe camping cottages, of which there are a few statewide, are almost identical to yurts in terms of amenities, even if they look more like a regular cabin.

Unique Houses

It's not often that you can stay in an old farmhouse, or even a mansion, with historic overtones. But those opportunities exist in Pennsylvania's state parks. The system has a dozen or so unique, always old, houses that are available for rent. They're typically bigger than the average cabin, with some sleeping a dozen people or more. All are full of modern features: full kitchens, regular beds, indoor plumbing, and the like; some even have fireplaces

At Pine Grove Furnace State Park you can rent the Paymaster's Cabin, a stone house that dates back to when an ironworks foundry existed on the site between 1764 and 1877. The Ironmaster's Mansion, the home of the man who ran the facility, also operates as a hostel. Built in 1829, it was reportedly a stop on the Underground Railroad for slaves escaping the South. Backpackers can stay at the mansion from April through December. It can also be rented for weddings and other events.

Visitors at Shawnee State Park can camp in a "lodge" overlooking the lake that sleeps eight and even has air-conditioning. In Trough Creek they can stay in another lodge that was built in the mid-1800s, again as an ironmaster's home.

The Inn at Cook Forest is a modern bed-and-breakfast. At Blue Knob State Park you can rent a cabin big enough to hold retreats. It sleeps one hundred persons in a bunkhouse-type atmosphere. It comes with a kitchen and dining hall too. Laurel Hill State Park has a lodge that sleeps fourteen and has one and a half kitchens that is popular with skiers; Raccoon Creek State Park has a ten-person lodge.

Bald Eagle State Park offers the Nature Inn—a full-service bed-and-breakfast that's really the park system's first and so far only hotel-like accommodations. It overlooks Sayers Lake and affords visitors single and double bedrooms and even suites, a library, children's discovery activities, some meals, and more. Not surprisingly it's the most expensive option when it comes to staying the night in a state park, but it appeals to some.

In all cases for all structures—cabins, cottages, yurts, and houses—reservations can be made by calling (888) 727-2757 or visiting pennsylvaniastateparks.reserveamerica .com/welcome.do.

Here's a look at state parks with cabins, cottages, yurts, and/or houses, broken down by region:

Facilities by Park

Western Pennsylvania

Keystone State Park: 11 modern cabins, 2 yurts, 3 camping cottages
Kooser State Park: 8 rustic cabins, 1 modern cabin
Laurel Hill State Park: Huffman Lodge, Copper Kettle Lodge, 8 camping cottages
Linn Run State Park: 1 modern cabin, 9 rustic cabins
Moraine State Park: 11 modern cabins
Ohiopyle State Park: 4 yurts, 6 camping cottages
Pymatuning State Park: 25 modern cabins
Raccoon Creek State Park: 10 modern cabins, the Lakeside Lodge
Ryerson Station State Park: 2 camping cottages, 3 deluxe camping cottages
Yellow Creek State Park: 4 yurts, 6 camping cottages

Northern Pennsylvania

Bald Eagle State Park: Nature Inn, 2 yurts, 3 camping cottages, 1 deluxe camping cottage
Black Moshannon State Park: 7 modern cabins, 13 rustic cabins, 2 deluxe camping cottages
Chapman State Park: 2 yurts, 3 camping cottages
Clear Creek State Park: 22 rustic cabins, 2 yurts
Cook Forest State Park: 20 rustic cabins, the Inn at Cook Forest
Hills Creek State Park: 10 modern cabins, 2 yurts, 3 camping cottages
Hyner Run State Park: two-story house
Little Pine State Park: 2 yurts, 3 camping cottages
Ole Bull State Park: 1.5-story log cabin
Parker Dam State Park: 17 rustic cabins, Parker Cabin
Simon B. Elliott State Park: 6 rustic cabins
Sinnemahoning State Park: two-story Brooks Run Cabin

Eastern Pennsylvania

Lackawanna State Park: 2 yurts, 3 camping cottages
Nockamixon State Park: 10 modern cabins
Promised Land State Park: 13 rustic cabins, 3 camping cottages
Ricketts Glen State Park: 10 modern cabins, 5 deluxe camping cottages
Tuscarora State Park: 4 yurts, 6 camping cottages
Worlds End State Park: 19 rustic cabins

Southern Pennsylvania

Blue Knob State Park: 3 modern cabins, Twin Fawn house

Caledonia State Park: 1 house

Canoe Creek State Park: 8 modern cabins

Codorus State Park: 2 yurts, 3 camping cottages

Cowans Gap State Park: 10 rustic cabins

French Creek State Park: 10 modern cabins, 2 yurts, 3 camping cottages

Gifford Pinchot State Park: 10 modern cabins, 2 yurts, 3 camping cottages

Hickory Run State Park: 3 camping cottages, 2 deluxe camping cottages

Little Buffalo State Park: 1 modern cabin, 4 camping cottages

Pine Grove Furnace State Park: Paymaster's Cabin, Ironmaster's Mansion hostel

Poe Paddy State Park: 5 Adirondack shelters

Poe Valley State Park: 3 camping cottages, 1 deluxe camping cottage

Prince Gallitzin State Park: 10 modern cabins, 3 camping cottages, 2 deluxe camping cottages

Raymond B. Winter State Park: 3 camping cottages

Shawnee State Park: Shawnee Lodge, 2 yurts, 3 camping cottages

Trough Creek State Park: Trough Creek Lodge

Allegheny National Forest also offers a few cabins for rent. You can find 11, all with electricity and sleeping four to six people, in Willow Bay Recreation Area. The national forest also rents the Farnsworth Cabin. Located about 8.5 miles northwest of Sheffield, it's another 1930s-era stone-and-wood house built by the CCC. Renovated in 2010 it features heat, air-conditioning, electricity, and even phone service. All forest cabins can be rented at recreation.gov.

Bucks County's Tohickon Valley Park offers four cabins for rent, two rustic and two modern. The modern ones, Cabins 3 and 4, were once private homes.

Two Mile Run County Park also rents two cottages.

Travel Tips

Wildlife

Pennsylvania is a wildlife lover's dream, uniquely positioned to be home to a wide variety of mammals, birds, and fish. White-tailed deer, gray and fox squirrels, ground-hogs, raccoons, skunks, black bears, bobcats, otters, fishers, coyotes, red and gray foxes, bald eagles, ospreys, red-tailed and sharp-shinned hawks, great horned owls, great blue herons—the state's got them all, often in good numbers.

Snowshoe hares, which are brown in summer and turn white in winter, can be found across the state's northern tier. Barn owls, which make a screaming, hissing sound rather than hooting like other owls, can be found especially in the agricultural south-central and southeast.

Your chances of seeing some of these species is greater now than at any time in the last century. Fishers, gone completely from Pennsylvania decades ago, were restocked in the northern portion of the state in the 1980s. Those animals have spread and linked up with other populations, reintroduced into West Virginia and New York by wildlife officials there at about the same time, so that they're now found across the northern and southwestern parts of Pennsylvania. That doesn't mean you'll see one of course. Fishers are shy animals and often nocturnal. But looking like the oversized weasels they are, they're a thrill to spot. They're interesting too in that they are the one predator that regularly preys on porcupines, which you'll also find in northern Pennsylvania.

Bobcat populations have similarly come back in the past four decades, and coy-ote numbers are booming. The latter are unique animals. Researchers at the State Museum of New York have determined that the eastern coyotes interbred with wolves many years ago, which accounts for their bigger size. A coyote in the western United States might top out at twenty pounds; in Pennsylvania and across the North-east, fifty-pounders are not unheard of.

Pennsylvania's elk herd, one of the largest east of the Mississippi, is a huge tourist draw. Fall weekends around places like Winslow Hill in Benezette Township in Elk County draw scads of tourists who come out to see some of the largest-racked elk in the world. Special viewing areas make the animals accessible—not that a giant bull elk lounging on the lawn of the local post office is hard to spot.

The presence of all of these critters requires some attention on your part, though.

Take black bears, for example. The state is home to an estimated 20,000 of them, spread across probably 90 percent of the state's sixty-seven counties. They're not equally distributed of course. The northern portion of the state, from Allegheny National Forest eastward, probably holds the most, with the area from the Laurel Highlands in southwestern Pennsylvania eastward across the south-central part of the state holding lots as well.

Pennsylvania's black bears start out small, like this eight-pound cub that was pulled from its den in March as part of a state-sponsored wildlife project. But they grow to be among the largest in the world, sometimes topping 800 pounds as adults.

The population is still growing and expanding its territory, so if black bears aren't in your favorite campground yet, just wait. They may show up sooner rather than later.

Black bears are not typically aggressive, so there's little to fear from them so long as you treat them as wild animals and follow the simple guidelines below when you're in the woods. There's no record of anyone being killed by a black bear in Pennsylvania in more than a century, and only twenty-five people have been injured by bears in the last decade or so.

But black bears are big, serious animals, capable of scrambling up a tree like a raccoon and sprinting like a racehorse, so you don't want to treat them as harmless either. And they can become troublesome if they get used to eating human food. You definitely don't want them in your tent. That's why at some campgrounds, park officials tell you to pack not only your food but also anything sweet-smelling, like toothpaste and deodorant, in your vehicle when preparing for bed or otherwise closing up your campsite at night.

If you encounter a bear that's being too inquisitive or that's making you feel uncomfortable, the Pennsylvania Game Commission, the agency responsible for managing the state's wildlife, recommends that you:

- Stay calm. If you see a bear and it hasn't seen you, leave the area calmly. Talk to the bear while moving away to help it discover your presence. Choose a route that will not intersect with the bear if it is moving.

- Get back. If you have surprised a bear, slowly back away while talking quietly. Face the bear, but avoid direct eye contact. Do not turn and run; rapid movement may be perceived as danger to a bear that is already feeling threatened or may trigger a prey response. Avoid blocking the bear's only escape route, and try to move away from any cubs you see or hear. Do not attempt to climb a tree. A female bear could interpret this as an attempt to get at her cubs, even though they may be in a different tree. Besides, black bears can climb better than you can. The most important thing to remember is to give any bear you encounter plenty of space. Don't crowd them to the point that they feel threatened and don't cut off their escape route.

- Pay attention. If a bear is displaying signs of nervousness or discomfort with your presence, such as pacing, swinging its head, or popping its jaws, leave the area. Some bears may bluff charge to within a few feet. If this occurs, stand your ground, wave your arms wildly above your head to make yourself look as big as possible, and shout at the bear. Turning and running could elicit a chase, and you cannot outrun a bear. Bears that appear to be stalking you should be confronted and made aware of your willingness to defend yourself by waving your arms and yelling while you continue to back away.

- Fight back. If a bear attacks, fight back as you continue to leave the area. Bears have been driven away with rocks, sticks, binoculars, car keys, or even bare hands.

Generally you can stay safe and enjoy wildlife without problems by treating the animals as the wild creatures they are. That means leaving bears, skunks, raccoons, and other critters to feed themselves. I'll never forget the time my wife, Mandy, and I took the kids camping and, just after crawling into the tent to unroll our sleeping bags, looked out to see four skunks just feet away. They were feeding on a bunch of sunflower seeds the previous camper had dumped on the ground at the base of a tree that was very near our tent door. We hadn't seen the seeds when setting up, but the skunks found them. By the time they'd had their fill and wandered away, the kids were asleep and we'd lost our evening.

The state is also home to three species of venomous snakes, with timber rattlers being the largest and most widespread. Like bears, they are generally unaggressive. If you hear a snake rattling, it's telling you to back away and leave it alone. Do that and you'll be fine.

The thing to remember in all cases is to let wildlife be wild. Animals that become habituated to people often get into trouble and end up being orphaned, relocated, or even killed. You can view wildlife, look at it, ooh and ah over it, love it, respect it, drool over it—but keep your hands off. That's the best thing for the animals in the long run.

The only wild thing you'll want to handle, and only when necessary, are ticks. Ticks use deer and more commonly mice as hosts but will latch onto people if the opportunity is there. They're a problem in Pennsylvania, which is one of the leading states for Lyme disease cases, with 3,000 to 4,000 confirmed each year.

Ticks need not keep you out of the woods. Just take precautions. To keep ticks at bay, use insect repellent and wear long pants and long-sleeved shirts when outdoors. Most importantly, be sure to check yourself whenever you come in after significant time outdoors. Especially check hard-to-see, dark, warm places, such as your crotch and around your hairline.

If you do find an embedded tick, remove it, and see a doctor when you get home. For tips on tick removal, visit the Lyme disease page of the Centers for Disease Control and Prevention website: cdc.gov/Lyme/.

Fishing and Hunting

Pennsylvania's public campgrounds afford countless opportunities to fish and hunt for all manner of species. Trout and bass are, in that order, the fish most commonly sought by anglers, but there are also muskies, northern pike, walleyes, catfish, and panfish to be caught. Hunters pursue white-tailed deer, black bears (the largest ever taken anywhere in the world by a hunter was killed in the Keystone State in 2011), elk, and small game from rabbits and squirrels to grouse and pheasants.

Licenses are required for both fishing and hunting.

Anglers 16 and older need to buy a fishing license from the Pennsylvania Fish and Boat Commission. You can buy them online at https://huntfish.pa.gov/or in person

A fly-fisherman casts his line into the Youghiogheny River in Ohiopyle State Park.

at thousands of vendors such as sporting goods stores, bait shops, and even hardware stores statewide. If you plan to fish for trout specifically, you'll also need a trout stamp; steelhead anglers and those fishing in Lake Erie need a Lake Erie permit. You can save some money and cover all your bases by purchasing a general fishing license and a combination trout/Erie stamp.

Nonresidents of the state can buy licenses good for the entire year or for periods as short as a few days. In all cases, for residents and nonresidents alike, the license year runs from January 1 to December 31.

While you're at it, visit the Fish and Boat Commission's website to get fishing tips; check out the county guide, which shows you where to fish and what you might find in various waters; and look at the calendar. It identifies where things like "family fishing programs"—which aim to teach people the basics of fishing—are being held. They're often scheduled for the same parks that have campgrounds.

When it comes to hunting, there are mentor programs where children and adults can try hunting without first buying a license. The rules cover only certain species, and there are guidelines about who can serve as a mentor, but it's a good way to introduce a newcomer to the activity. Eventually, to continue they need to buy a license. Children ages 12 to 16 can hunt with a junior license; those 17 and older need an adult license. A general license, or "back tag," allows you to hunt antlered deer and small game. Special additional licenses are needed if you want to hunt with a bow or muzzleloader; hunt bears, elk, bobcats, or fishers; or trap. Licenses are available at https://huntfish.pa.gov/ or at vendors statewide. A visit to the website also reveals where and when pheasants will be stocked, gives season dates and bag limits, and more.

Nonresident hunting licenses are available, including those good for a complete year or for as little as seven days. In all cases the nonresident license year runs from July 1 to June 30.

Hunting is not permitted in campgrounds or in the day-use area of most parks, so if you're not involved in hunting yourself, you'll probably never even come across a hunter. If you do venture farther afield during hunting season, primarily fall, wear clothing that makes you easily visible. Hunters wear bright orange; you should too.

Boating

Many of Pennsylvania's public campgrounds are in parks with lakes or situated along rivers. That makes it easy to combine a campout with some wonderful boating.

There are some rules to keep in mind though. Motorboats—even those equipped only with an electric motor—must be registered with the Pennsylvania Fish and Boat Commission. Nonpowered boats such as rowboats, canoes, and kayaks do not need to be registered. But if you plan to launch a nonpowered boat at a state park or a commission-owned access, you will need a launch permit. They're available from the commission or state park offices.

Pennsylvania is home to more than two dozen water trails, as well as smaller creeks, ponds, larger lakes, and every other waterway you can imagine.

Certain bodies of water have specific rules unique to them. Some lakes have horsepower restrictions: 10 horsepower at some lakes, 20 at others. Boating on Lake Erie requires you to carry more safety equipment, like flares, than elsewhere in the state. On lakes managed by the US Army Corps Pittsburgh District, everyone must wear a life jacket at all times when in canoes, kayaks, and other watercraft less than 16 feet in length.

State Fish and Boat Commission rules state that children younger than 12 must wear life jackets at all times in boats less than 20 feet. However, because of the danger of cold water, from November 1 to April 30 anyone out in a canoe, kayak, or boat less than 16 feet, regardless of age, must wear a life jacket at all times, whether under way or at anchor.

Where to boat? The commission has partnered with a number of organizations to develop official "water trails" around the state. These are paths along rivers and streams that have been marked and plotted just like hiking trails. Trail guides for each show access points for getting on and off the water; identify riffles, rapids, and other potential hazards; point out historic sites you'll pass along the way; provide information about the fish to be caught and the wildlife to be seen; and even highlight locations where you can do some dispersed camping.

The maps and guides are all very well done, in my experience. Some are available free from the commission; others must be purchased from its partners. Some of the trails are floatable year-round; others are passable only at times of high water in spring. Some are designed specifically for canoers and kayakers; others are on water big enough to handle larger boats. All are fun and worth exploring.

No matter where you boat, consider taking a boating safety education class before your first venture. Successfully passing the class is a prerequisite for operating a motorboat for anyone born after 1982. More importantly for everyone, the course will teach you the "rules of the road" on the water and perhaps save your life.

Finally, be sure to clean all of your boating gear—as well as your fishing equipment—before moving from one waterway to another. That will help slow the spread of invasive aquatic species, which are a real problem in Pennsylvania and elsewhere. Didymo, or rock snot—yes, it looks every bit as uninviting as the name suggests—is not native to the Keystone State and in fact can harm its waters and the fish, invertebrates, and insects that live in them by covering stream and river bottoms with slime. It's been found in two Pennsylvania waterways already: parts of the Delaware and Youghiogheny Rivers.

Fish and Boat Commission officials aren't sure they can get didymo out of those places. But they are asking boaters and anglers to be aware that it's there, and perhaps elsewhere, and take steps to keep it from spreading.

To do your part, drain your boat or bilge of any water before you leave a site. Wash your gear—boats, life jackets, anchors and line, skis and tubes, live wells, bait buckets, paddles, waders, shoes, and such—in water that's been heated to at least 140 degrees. A pressure washer at a commercial car wash is a good bet. And be sure to completely dry any gear before moving from one waterway to another.

Remove any visible mud, plants, and animals from your gear, but don't rely exclusively on a visual inspection. Some of these invasive species can exist and move about as a single cell, so a visual test alone isn't good enough.

Camping Etiquette

In my old Boy Scout troop, we had a mantra: Leave every campsite better than you found it. Too few people live up to that standard. If you've ever pulled into your campsite, wanted to build a fire, and first had to empty the fire circle of bars of soap, toothpaste tubes, Styrofoam plates that didn't burn or melt, scraps of aluminum foil, those chemical hand warmers, and the like or had to clean your tent pad of food wrappers, plastic cups, and other debris, you know what I mean.

Nobody wants to have to clean up after the previous camper, so either dispose of your garbage—many campgrounds have a common dumpster—or at least bag it up and take it out with you.

CAMP ANF-3
1933 - 1946
FOREST SERVICE
U S
DEPARTMENT OF AGRICULTURE
Chapter 125
New Castle, PA
CCC Alumni and
Wilcox Friends
UNITED STATES
CCC
CIVILIAN CONSERVATION CORPS
The Civilian Conservation Corps established Camp ANF-3 near this location in 1933 at the height of the Great Depression. Enrollees lived here and worked on various conservation projects within the Allegheny National Forest. The camp later housed World War II German prisoners of war between 1943 and 1946.
ALLEGHENY
National Forest

It's important to be respectful of the state's many public campgrounds for many reasons, not the least of which is that some occupy or sit adjacent to historic sites. The former Camp ANF-3, near Red Bridge Recreation Area, was home to Civilian Conservation Corps workers during America's Great Depression and to German prisoners of war during World War II.

Here are some Leave No Trace principles to keep in mind:

- Plan ahead and prepare.
- Know the regulations and special concerns for the area you'll visit.
- Prepare for extreme weather, hazards, and emergencies.
- Schedule your trip to avoid times of high use.
- Visit in small groups when possible. Consider splitting larger groups into smaller ones.
- Repackage food to minimize waste.
- Use a map and compass to eliminate the use of marking paint, rock cairns, or flagging.
- Travel and camp on durable surfaces such as established trails and campsites, rock, gravel, dry grasses, or snow.

- Protect riparian areas by camping at least 200 feet from lakes and streams.
- Don't alter a site. Good campsites are found, not made.
- In popular areas concentrate use on existing trails and campsites.
- Walk single file in the middle of the trail, even when it's wet or muddy.
- Keep campsites small. Focus activity in areas without vegetation.
- Disperse use in pristine areas to prevent creating new campsites and trails; avoid places where impacts are just beginning.
- Dispose of waste properly: Pack it in; pack it out. Inspect your campsite and rest areas for trash or spilled foods. Pack out all trash, leftover food, and litter.
- If you are somewhere without restrooms, deposit solid human waste in cat holes dug 6 to 8 inches deep at least 200 feet from water, campsites, and trails. Cover and disguise the cat hole when finished.
- Pack out toilet paper and other hygiene products.
- To wash yourself or your dishes, carry water 200 feet away from streams or lakes and use small amounts of biodegradable soap. Scatter strained dishwater.
- Leave what you find. Preserve the past: Examine but do not touch cultural or historic structures and artifacts.
- Leave rocks, plants, and other natural objects as you find them.
- Avoid introducing or transporting nonnative species.
- Do not build structures or furniture and do not dig trenches.
- Minimize campfires, which can cause lasting impacts to the backcountry. Use a lightweight stove for cooking, and enjoy a candle lantern for light.
- Where fires are permitted, use established fire rings, fire pans, or mound fires.
- Keep fires small. Only use sticks from the ground that can be broken by hand.
- Burn all wood and coals to ash; put out campfires completely and then scatter cool ashes.
- Respect wildlife by observing it from a distance. Do not follow or approach it.
- Never feed wild animals. Feeding wildlife damages their health, alters natural behaviors, and exposes them to predators and other dangers.
- Protect wildlife and your food by storing rations and trash securely.
- Avoid wildlife during sensitive times: mating and nesting seasons, when animals are raising young, or in winter.
- Be courteous. Yield to other users on the trail.
- Step to the downhill side of the trail when encountering pack stock.
- Take breaks and camp away from trails and other visitors.
- Let nature's sounds prevail. Avoid loud voices and noises.
  For more information visit LNT.org.

In addition to these guidelines, be considerate of your neighbors and observe the posted quiet times within a campground. The rules don't say you have to go to bed at a particular time. But if quiet time is 10 p.m. to 6 a.m., don't be hooting and hollering at 2 a.m. Don't monopolize the facilities either. If you've got wet clothes, for example, string a clothesline rather than draping them over the bathroom facilities everyone has to share.

And if you've got the family dog along, and the rules say he must be leashed, don't turn him loose to roam the campground. Your pet not only could get hurt by a passing vehicle but also could ruin the stay of others.

Camping with Kids

There are all kinds of real, tangible benefits—mental, physical, and social—to getting children outdoors and exploring nature; it's just great fun too. The memories you'll make fishing, paddling a canoe, hiking a trail, investigating leaves and bugs that you find, or counting the stars with your children are ones you will cherish forever.

There are some things you'll want to keep in mind to make any outing a successful one, though:

Get the kids involved. Long before you leave home, allow the kids to help plan your "adventure." Look at park maps before you go, and get the kids involved in picking a campground and a site within it. Ask what they want to do while they are there, and then work together to pack everything from your fishing equipment to sleeping bags. Giving kids some ownership of the trip builds excitement.

Get them their own gear. From a practical standpoint you might be able to light up your campsite with one lantern. But the kids will have more fun if you let them each wear their own headlamp or carry their own flashlight, water bottle, or small backpack. You need not spend a lot of money on their gear initially; they'll outgrow some of it anyway. But if they have their own "stuff," they are more likely to feel like a camper.

Keep it simple. As adults we sometimes get hard core. We want to bike a top trail or fish a famous stream or marvel at a spectacular overlook. Kids want to have fun too, but their attention spans are shorter. Keep that in mind when you go camping, and let them set the pace. They may fish for an hour then tire of it and want to hit the playground. A 30-minute hike might be better for them than a daylong trek. Canoeing around the lake might need to be broken up with time spent looking for bugs. Remember, you're out here to get away from schedules. Be flexible.

Explore the little things. When you camp with kids, it's always a good idea to spend time looking for fancy rocks, bugs, pinecones, and animal tracks. All of nature is new to children; be sure to discover it with them. And be enthusiastic about their finds. You want to build excitement in them.

Take more than one. The goal on any camping trip with children is to make sure they have fun; that will make them want to come back for more. So consider letting your children take along a friend. They'll keep each other occupied and happy.

Make food fun. The old standby, the hot dog cooked on a stick over a fire, may not be the most appealing thing to the chefs among us, but kids love fires and cooking over them. Let them be involved, and let them make things they don't get to make at home. Mountain pies are great, as are s'mores. One of those ice-cream makers that you work by shaking is fun, too.

Let others help. Many parks offer environmental education programs aimed specifically at children. Call ahead to the park you'll be visiting and see what they might have on tap. Even if there's not a program scheduled per se, sometimes you can make arrangements to stop by a nature center and spend time with a ranger or educator who can let children touch animal hides, tell you where in the park to see wildlife, or otherwise help gain kids' interest.

Have fun. The most important thing to remember when camping is to have fun. If you stress out on a campout or complain about how far the bathroom is from the tent or whine about sleeping on the ground, your kids will feed off that vibe. It's up to you to set the tone. When my children were little, we never went on "walks"; we always went on "adventures." The idea was to make them understand that being outdoors was a grand experience, something to be cherished. Be positive. Be adventurous. Be fun.

So gather up the gang, grab your fishing rods and swimming suits, put on your sunscreen, and head outdoors. You'll be glad you did.

Tourism Information and Things to See and Do

In many cases the parks surrounding your public campground will have plenty to keep you busy. There will be swimming, hiking, fishing, playgrounds, boating, and more. But that's not all there is to the state. There are many, many state and federal parks and wildlife refuges worth exploring that offer no camping, historical sites ranging from Valley Forge National Historical Park to Gettysburg National Military Park, attractions from the wildlife-focused Elk Country Visitor Center to Pittsburgh's Western Pennsylvania Sports Museum and amusement parks, railroad museums, and famous eateries. Telling you about them all is the job of Pennsylvania's Department of Community and Economic Development. It's the state's official tourism bureau. Check out its website: www.visitpa.com.

The department breaks the state down into eleven regions, compared to the Department of Conservation and Natural Resources' four, so things can get a little confusing when it comes to linking the location of your campground to other attractions. Not all of the eleven fit neatly into those four either.

Generally speaking, the boundaries of Pennsylvania's Great Lakes Region, Pittsburgh and its Countryside, and the Laurel Highlands areas match those for campgrounds in the West. The boundaries of The Alleghenies and Dutch Country Roads are tied to the South region campgrounds. The area known as the Pennsylvania Wilds is largely tied to campgrounds in the North, while Philadelphia and its Countryside, the Lehigh Valley, the Pocono Mountains, and Upstate PA are largely related to the campgrounds in the East.

Exploring the tourism bureau's website is worthwhile, especially if you're looking to do a multiday, multipark camping excursion. It details road trips of interest, for example, so that the drive between parks can be fun and filled with places to eat, shop, and explore. The website will even suggest road trips tied to history, outdoor adventure, the arts, and other topics of interest. You can also get directions, information on special deals, and details on special events like fairs, festivals, craft shows, and museum days.

You may already know what you want to do and where, and that's OK. A visit to the website may reveal opportunities you were not aware of, even close to a campground you've been visiting for years. It's worth a look anyway!

Map Legend

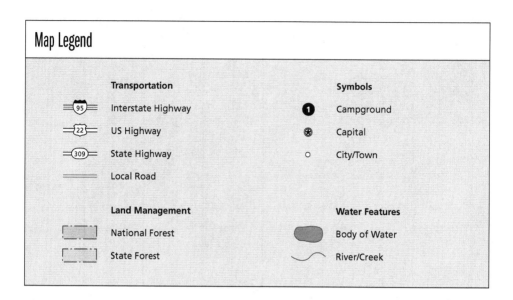

Transportation

═⟨95⟩═	Interstate Highway
═⟨22⟩═	US Highway
═⟨309⟩═	State Highway
═══════	Local Road

Land Management

[░░░]	National Forest
[░░░]	State Forest

Symbols

❶	Campground
✪	Capital
○	City/Town

Water Features

⬬	Body of Water
∿	River/Creek

Western
Pennsylvania
Mountains, Lakes, and Hills

Fall colors are reflected in Raccoon Lake at Raccoon Creek State Park.

Western Pennsylvania can be divided into three regions, each with its own distinct personality.

The northernmost part is known as Pennsylvania's Great Lakes Region for its frontage on Lake Erie. That brings some of the best stream steelhead fishing in the nation; terrific lake fishing for smallmouth bass, walleyes, and panfish; swimming at Erie's beaches; lighthouses to visit; and an amazing abundance of birdlife.

There's more to this region than just Lake Erie though. This is a land of glacial lakes, man-made reservoirs like Pymatuning—where you can feed carp that congregate in such numbers that the "ducks walk on the fish"—and streams like French Creek, one of the most ecologically rich waters in the Northeast as well as a great place to paddle. You can also tour a winery, visit one of Pennsylvania's three national wildlife refuges, or visit towns like Franklin that are long on Victorian houses and charm.

At the other end of this region lie the Laurel Highlands. Located on the westernmost edge of the Appalachian Mountains, this is the place for high adventure. The Youghiogheny (pronounced yawk-o-GAY-knee) River slices through, flowing north and offering some of the best whitewater rafting in the East where it passes through Ohiopyle State Park. The region also contains the 150-mile Great Allegheny Passage bike trail, waterfalls, mountain headwater stream brook trout fishing, caverns, and hiking.

If you want to slow things down a bit, there's history to see at Fort Necessity, the site of George Washington's only surrender. Nearby you can explore world-renowned architecture in the form of Fallingwater and Kentuck Knob, homes built by Frank Lloyd Wright, and take a scenic drive along US 40, called the "National Road" because it was the country's first federally funded highway.

In between those two regions lies Pittsburgh, the state's second-largest city; around it is a surprising amount of open space. Pittsburgh offers all that you'd expect: professional football, baseball, and hockey teams; art and natural history museums; a zoo; a history center; and shopping. There are bridges aplenty too. The Allegheny and Monongahela Rivers meet to form the Ohio—the "three rivers" in local parlance—at what's called "The Point." The result is 440-plus bridges, more than crisscross just about any other city in the world.

To the west you'll find a land of rolling—and rolling and rolling and rolling—hills. In Ryerson Station State Park on the West Virginia border, the landscape seems to be made up of green, wooded waves, steep if not tall, so that you need one leg longer than the other to get around without trouble.

Simply put, there's a lot of variety. There's camping offered at state parks, US Army Corps of Engineers impoundments, and even one large county park. So whether you prefer your adventure on the water, in the woods, or close to the city, you can find what you're looking for. Go have fun!

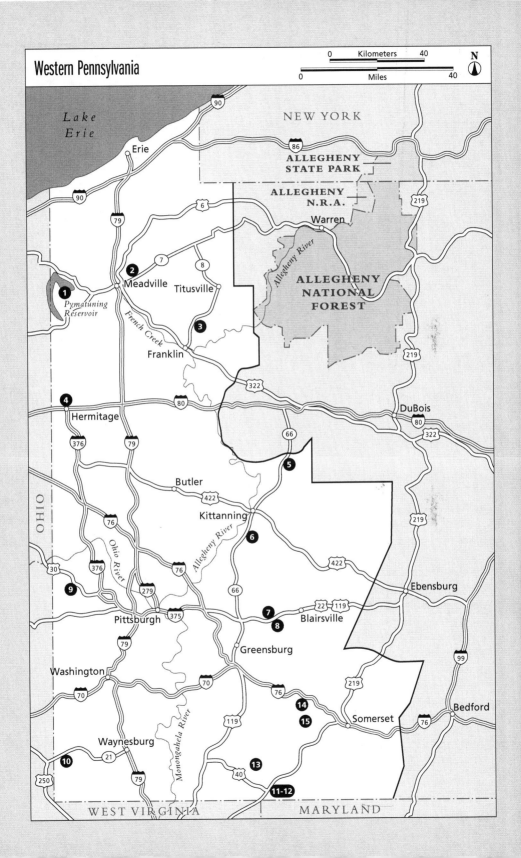

Park	Total Sites	Hookups	Max RV Length	Toilets	Showers	Drinking Water	Dump Station	Recreation	Fee	Reservation
1. Pymatuning State Park	401	Y	60/45	F	Y	Y	Y	H, B, F, S, C, L, EE, U	$$$–$$$$	Y
2. Colonel Crawford Park	111	Y	60	F	Y	Y	Y	H, B, F, S, L, U	$$$–$$$$	Y
3. Two Mile Run County Park	72	Y	40	F	Y	Y	Y	H, B, F, S, C, L, R, EE, U	$$–$$$$	Y
4. Shenango River Lake	321	Y	80	F	Y	Y	Y	H, B, F, L, U, O	$$$–$$$$	Y
5. Mahoning Creek Lake–Milton Loop Campground	54	Y	70	F	Y	Y	Y	H, B, F, L, U	$$$–$$$$	Y
6. Crooked Creek Lake	45	Y	35	F	Y	Y	Y	B, F, S, L, R, EE, U	$–$$	Y
7. Loyalhanna Lake	44	Y	60	F	Y	Y	Y	H, B, F, C, L, U	$$$–$$$$	Y
8. Keystone State Park	100	Y	55	F	Y	Y	Y	H, B, F, S, C, L, EE, U	$$$–$$$$	Y
9. Raccoon Creek State Park	172	Y	40	F	Y	Y	Y	H, B, F, S, C, L, EE, U	$$$–$$$$	Y
10. Ryerson Station State Park	35	Y	40	V	Y	Y	Y	H, F, C, EE, U	$$$–$$$$	Y
11. Youghiogheny River Lake Outflow Campground	64	Y	64	F	Y	Y	Y	H, B, F, S, C, L, U	$$–$$$$	Y
12. Youghiogheny River Lake Yough Lake Campground	101	Y	55	F	Y	Y	Y	H, B, F, S, C, L, U	$$$–$$$$	Y
13. Ohiopyle State Park	209	Y	40	F	Y	Y	Y	H, B, F, C, L, EE, U	$$$–$$$$	Y
14. Kooser State Park	35	Y	40	F	Y	Y	Y	H, F, S, C	$$$–$$$$	Y
15. Laurel Hill State Park	264	Y	40	F	Y	Y	Y	H, B, F, S, L, EE, U	$$$–$$$$	Y

Y = yes, N = no
Toilets: F = flush, V = vault
Recreation: H = hiking, B = boating, F = fishing, S = swimming, C = cycling, L = boat launch, R = horseback riding, EE = environmental education, U = hunting; O = off-road vehicle area.
Fee: $ to $$$$

1 Pymatuning State Park

Location: West of Meadville
Season: Mid-Apr through mid-Oct
Sites: 401, some ADA accessible, in two campgrounds: Jamestown Campground on the south shore and Linesville Campground on the north shore. A third campground that has been long closed, Tuttle, is expected to reopen early in 2022.
Maximum RV length: 60 feet at Jamestown, 45 feet at Linesville
Facilities: Flush toilets, warm showers, water, sanitary dump station, electricity, coin-operated laundry, camp stores, picnic tables, fire rings, boat launch and rentals
Fee per night: $$$–$$$$
Pets: Permitted at some sites
Activities: Swimming, scenic vistas, spillway concession, boating, fishing, hunting, hiking, disc golf
Management: Pennsylvania Department of Conservation and Natural Resources
Contact: (724) 932-3142; www.dcnr.state.pa.us/stateparks/findapark/pymatuning/index.htm. For reservations call toll-free (888) 727-2757 or visit VisitPaParks.com.
Finding the campground: From Meadville go west on US 322 for 8.5 miles. At the Y with US 6, turn left (south) onto US 322 and go 11.7 miles. Turn right onto US 322 and go another 2 miles to reach Jamestown. To reach Linesville turn right at the Y with US 6 and follow it.
GPS coordinates: N41 51.611'/W80 50.472' for Jamestown; N41 65.691'/W80 46.170' for Linesville
Other: This park rents 25 modern cabins and has an organized group tenting area.
About the campground: The Jamestown Campground is the much larger of the two and the more crowded. Combined, the two campgrounds offer 52 full hookup (sewage, water, electric, 30/50 amp) sites, more than any other state park. There are watercraft concessions and marinas near both campgrounds, so you can rent boats by the hour, day, or even week if you don't have your own.
Why it's worth a visit: Pymatuning Lake is the main attraction and no wonder: At more than 17,000 acres, it accounts for most of the park's total of 21,000 acres. In fact it's the largest impoundment in the state. There's still room to hike—there are more than 7 miles of trails—but boating, swimming, and fishing for the lake's abundant walleyes, crappies, muskies, and bass are the main draws. Be sure to check out the famous Linesville Spillway, where giant carp by the tens of thousands—and ducks, geese, and gulls that walk on the backs of the fish—crowd the shore to eat bread tossed by spectators. There's a concession stand too, so it's a nice place to spend some time, especially with children. This area is also home to Pennsylvania's densest concentration of bald eagles, so be sure to watch for them. The area around the spillway and the Pennsylvania Fish and Boat Commission's Linesville state fish hatchery is a good spot to see eagles, as well as deer and geese.

2 Colonel Crawford Park

Location: North of Meadville
Season: Memorial Day through Labor Day
Sites: 111
Maximum RV length: 60 feet

Facilities: Flush toilets, warm showers, water, electricity, sanitary dump station, picnic tables, fire rings, grills, boat launch, playground, visitor center (open on weekends), scenic overlook

Fee per night: $$$–$$$$

Pets: Leashed pets permitted

Activities: Swimming, fishing, boating, hiking, hunting, picnic shelters. There is also an 18-hole disc golf course on the outflow side of Woodcock Dam accessible via the Outflow Recreation Area.

Management: US Army Corps of Engineers, Pittsburgh District

Contact: (814) 763-4422; www.lrp.usace.army.mil/Missions/Recreation/Lakes/Woodcock-Creek -Lake/. For reservations call toll-free (877) 444-6777 or visit recreation.gov. There are some first-come, first-served campsites.

Finding the campground: From Meadville follow Hickory Street / Route 77 north for 0.7 mile. Take the first left onto Dickson Street and go 2.7 miles. Take a slight right onto Shultz Road; go 0.8 mile and take the first left into the park.

GPS coordinates: N41 69.097' / W80 08.278'

Other: This US Army Corps of Engineers Lake is the largest recreational facility in Crawford County.

About the campground: The campground is a series of loops near the causeway.

Why it's worth a visit: Like most Corps facilities, the 333-acre Woodcock Creek Lake offers fine fishing for muskies, northern pike, panfish, walleyes, and largemouth and smallmouth bass. Unlike the state's other Corps-managed lakes, though, this one is small enough that there's a 10-horsepower limit in effect for boats. That means no competition from speedboaters while you're casting a line. There is a six-lane boat launch, so there's not a lot of waiting to get on the water. If you prefer coldwater fishing, Woodcock Creek is stocked above and below the dam with trout in spring. If you want to keep your feet on solid ground, Bossard Nature Study Trail, located on the north side of the lake, has markers identifying 198 tree and shrub species and two observation blinds where you can sit and watch for wildlife. About 1,000 feet of the trail is paved. Hikers, walkers, and joggers can also follow an access road that traverses the top of the dam, nearly 1 mile across, to enjoy some spectacular views.

3 Two Mile Run County Park

Location: North of Oil City

Season: Mid-May to mid-Oct

Sites: 72; 7 walk-in only; 3 walk-in or boat-in only, each with their own docks; and 2 boat-in only sites

Maximum RV length: 40 feet within the campground; larger ones accommodated adjacent to the nature lodge in the off-season camping area.

Facilities: Flush toilets, warm showers, water, electric, sanitary dump station, picnic tables, fire rings, nature center, boat rental, athletic fields, numerous playgrounds, and 2 boat launches

Fee per night: $$–$$$$

Pets: Leashed pets permitted

Activities: Fishing, boating, swimming, hiking, mountain biking, equestrian trails, hunting

Management: Venango County

Contact: www.co.venango.pa.us/152/Parks-Recreation. For reservations call (814) 676-6116 or (888) TWO-MILE.

Finding the campground: From Franklin, take state route 417 north for 6.5 miles. Turn right onto Baker Road and follow it for 2 miles to Cherrytree Road. Take a slight left onto Cherrytree Road and go 1 mile before turning right onto Beach Road. Follow for 1 mile to the park office.

GPS coordinates: N41 47.951'/W79 75.920'

Other: There is a 1929 farmhouse and a 1950 cottage for rent. Book early, though; they sometimes rent a year in advance. An equestrian camping area is also available.

About the campground: The walk-in, lakeside sites are the most rustic and spacious. Three sites offer boat tie-ups.

Why it's worth a visit: At 2,695 acres this is a huge park by county standards, so there's lots to do and plenty of space to do it in. In recent seasons one of the major attractions has been the park's many nature programs. They include everything from guided nighttime, full-moon nature hikes to wildlife presentations, a regatta, and tree and bird identification programs. This park is also popular with horseback riders and mountain bikers. Horseback riders can take part in a regular, full schedule of trail rides from June through October. Bikers will find more than 30 miles of single- and double-track trails that challenge riders with creek crossings, bridges, rocks, roots, logs, and rolling hills. An 18-plus-mile bike race is held here each summer. Fishermen also make heavy use of the park year-round, pursuing trout, bass, panfish, and walleyes in Justus Lake, also known as Two Mile Run Reservoir.

4 Shenango River Lake

Location: South of Greenville

Season: Mid-May to mid-Sept

Sites: 321

Maximum RV length: 80 feet

Facilities: Flush toilets, warm showers, sanitary dump station, water, electricity, picnic tables, fire rings, boat launches, off-road vehicle area

Fee per night: $$$–$$$$

Pets: Leashed pets permitted

Activities: Hiking, fishing, hunting, boating, waterskiing, tubing, swimming, off-roading

Management: US Army Corps of Engineers, Pittsburgh District

Contact: (724) 962-7746; www.lrp.usace.army.mil/Missions/Recreation/Lakes/Shenango-River -Lake/. For reservations call toll-free (877) 444-6777 or visit www.recreation.gov. There are some first-come, first-served campsites.

Finding the campground: From Greenville follow Route 18 south. Just before crossing the bridge over Shenango Reservoir, turn right onto West Lake Road; continue about 1.25 miles to the campground.

GPS coordinates: N41 29.948'/W80 43.709'

Other: History buffs will enjoy exploring the remnants of the Erie Extension Canal, which played a key role in the economic development of this part of the state. Sections of the extension are located here and maintained for hiking as part of the Shenango Trail. The well-preserved remains of Lock Number 10 are located in Sharpsville, 0.5 mile downstream of the dam. Another historic feature worth checking out is the Kidd's Mill Covered Bridge.

An angler holds a large crappie pulled from the waters of Shenango Lake, a US Army Corps of Engineers facility.

About the campground: This large modern campground is broken down Into four sections. Some of the nicest, and closest to the water, are situated on a peninsula.

Why it's worth a visit: Like most Army Corps of Engineers lakes, Shenango allows unlimited-horsepower boating and so is very popular for waterskiing and tubing as well as fishing. For a different experience take your canoe or kayak and explore some of the lake's more remote areas. You can also go upstream and float the Shenango River. A water trail has been developed that runs from Pymatuning State Park to Big Bend, which is the easternmost end of this recreation area. This is a nice, relaxing Class I float suitable for beginner paddlers.

Another thing that makes this park unique is the Bayview Off-Road Vehicle Area for all-terrain vehicles. Truth be told, public lands open to ATVs are scarce in this part of the state. The Bayview Area is open from late May through the end of September. There are some rules to follow: No one younger than 8 can ride, and those 8 to 15 must first pass a safety education course. If you meet those standards, this is a good place to visit.

5 Mahoning Creek Lake-Milton Loop Campground

Location: North of Dayton
Season: Apr 1 through Oct 31
Sites: 54
Maximum RV length: 70 feet
Facilities: Flush toilets, warm showers, water, electricity, sanitary dump station, picnic tables, fire rings, boat launch, playground
Fee per night: $$$-$$$$
Pets: Leashed pets permitted
Activities: Boating, fishing, hiking, hunting
Management: Armstrong County
Contact: (814) 257-8811 or www.lrp.usace.army.mil/Missions/Recreation/Lakes/Mahoning -Creek-Lake/ for information about the lake. For campground information or reservations call (814) 257-0131 or facebook.com/gearhartsmiltonloopcampground/. There are some first-come, first-served campsites at certain times.
Finding the campground: From Dayton head northeast on Route 839 for about 2.5 miles. Just before reaching Milton turn left at the signs into the campground.
GPS coordinates: N40 90.415' / W79 22.155'
Other: There are a few small cabins for rent. This is also a fishing rod and tackle loaner site; visitors who stop by the Army Corps office can sign out a rod and tackle box stocked with hooks and other gear for up to three days at a time with photo identification.
About the campground: This campground is run by a private concessionaire. Most of the sites here are relatively open, in grassy areas near a woodline.
Why it's worth a visit: This lake, located among steep-sided, wooded hills, is a favorite of paddlers and other small boat owners because it restricts boats to no more than 10 horsepower. The various bays, inlets, and other nooks and crannies upstream and down of the campground offer some spectacular scenery, especially when the hills are ablaze in fall color, and are tranquil and fun to explore. Paddling here is more comparable to floating a wide, lazy river—which of course it is—than paddling a big lake. The fishing is pretty good too, especially for bass, walleyes, channel catfish, panfish, and northern pike. The outflow area has a fishing pier for those with special needs. If you want to hike, a portion of the 141-mile Baker Trail passes through the campground. There's also a wildlife area nearby.

6 Crooked Creek Lake

Location: South of Kittanning
Season: Mid-May to early Oct
Sites: 45
Maximum RV length: 35 feet
Facilities: Restrooms within the park (though not within the campground itself), water, sanitary dump station at park office, picnic tables, fire rings, playground, boat launch, environmental learning center (www.armstrongcenter.org/locations/odc/), horse park

A young man rides a personal watercraft at Crooked Creek Lake, a US Army Corps of Engineers—managed lake north of Pittsburgh.

Fee per night: $-$$

Pets: Leashed pets permitted

Activities: Boating, waterskiing, tubing, swimming, hiking, horseback riding, fishing, hunting

Management: US Army Corps of Engineers, Pittsburgh District

Contact: (724) 763-3161; www.lrp.usace.army.mil/missions/recreation/lakes/crooked-creek -lake/. For reservations call toll-free (877) 444-6777 or visit recreation.gov.

Finding the campground: From Kittanning head south on Route 66 for 7 miles. Shortly after passing the entrance to the main day-use area, turn left onto Boat Launch Road and follow signs to the campground.

GPS coordinates: N40 70.842' / W79 51.638'

Other: Crooked Creek rangers and local historians developed Crooked Creek's "auto tour trail," which takes in the local history of Armstrong County.

About the campground: This is a rustic campground close to Pittsburgh. Alcoholic beverages are prohibited.

Why it's worth a visit: This lake's beach, which sits on a peninsula, is very popular with swimmers. The ADA-accessible fishing pier in the outflow area is a major attraction for anglers. The lake itself is a favorite with powerboaters, who zip up and down it while anglers work its shorelines.

Two things are especially interesting about this area. One is the horse park operated by Fort Armstrong Horsemen's Association. Located on 100 acres within the park, it's not a public facility where you can rent horses. But you can see horse shows and rodeos and, if you have your own animal, take part in clinics and ride trails. About 40 miles of marked trails climb hills, cross streams, and wind through the woods. Maps are available at the park's information center.

The other interesting feature is the Crooked Creek Environmental Learning Center. More than just a traditional nature center, it maintains trails and offers guided hikes, provides weeklong nature programs for children, hosts field trips, offers geocaching, and showcases mounts of local mammals, birds, fish, and reptiles. There's an herb garden too.

7 Loyalhanna Lake

Location: South of Saltsburg

Season: Early May through mid-September

Sites: 44

Maximum RV length: 60 feet

Facilities: Flush toilets, warm showers, water, electricity, sanitary dump station, picnic tables, fire rings, lantern hangers, playground, volleyball court, boat launches, boat trail

Fee per night: $$$-$$$$

Pets: Leashed pets permitted

Activities: Fishing, boating, hiking, biking (along West Penn Trail), hunting

Management: US Army Corps of Engineers, Pittsburgh District

Contact: (724) 369-9013; www.lrp.usace.army.mil/Missions/Recreation/Lakes/Loyalhanna -Lake/. For reservations call toll-free (877) 444-6777 or visit recreation.gov.

Finding the campground: From Saltsburg follow Route 981 south for a little less than 1 mile. Turn left onto Bush Road and go about 3 miles to the campground.

GPS coordinates: N40 43.991' / W79 43.433'

Other: The West Penn Trail, a 17-mile multiuse path that's great for biking, follows the former right-of-way of the Pennsylvania Main Line Canal and West Penn Railroad. The trail can be accessed at the Corps' nearby Conemaugh Lake facility.

About the campground: About half the sites here are in a mostly wooded area; the other half are more open. There's also a group tenting site. Alcoholic beverages are prohibited.

Why it's worth a visit: This is another lake with no horsepower restrictions, but when you're ready to slow down a bit, there's a self-guided water trail called the Black Willow Water Trail. Suitable for canoes as well as larger boats, it takes you to specific features, some man-made, some natural, where you might observe wildlife or be able to study the exotic erosion patterns of headwater sandstone cliffs. A trail brochure available at the ranger booth at Bush Recreation Area offers details. The campground is located adjacent to the boat launch ramp at that same site.

There's also a lot of hunting to be found here. The Corps leases nearly 3,000 acres to the Pennsylvania Game Commission, which manages it for species such as white-tailed deer, turkeys, rabbits, squirrels, and pheasants. A call to the Corps office will get you a map that shows parking and access areas for hunters.

8 Keystone State Park

Location: East of Murrysville
Season: First Fri in Apr through third Sun in Oct
Sites: 100, some ADA accessible, in two campground loops: Lakeside and Hillside
Maximum RV length: 55 feet
Facilities: Flush toilets, warm showers, water, electricity, sanitary dump station, picnic tables, fire rings, boat rental
Fee per night: $$$-$$$$
Pets: Permitted at some sites
Activities: Swimming, boating, fishing, hunting, environmental education programs, biking, hiking
Management: Pennsylvania Department of Conservation and Natural Resources
Contact: (724) 668-2939; www.dcnr.state.pa.us/stateparks/findapark/keystone/index.htm. For reservations call toll-free (888) 727-2757 or visit VisitPaParks.com.
Finding the campground: From Murrysville follow US 22 east for 15 miles. Turn right (south) onto Route 981; go 0.3 mile and turn left onto Keystone Park Road. Go 2.6 miles; turn right onto Slag Road, continuing until you reach the campground entrance.
GPS coordinates: N40 37.242'/W79 38.616' for Lakeside; N40 37.340'/W79 39.409' for Hillside
Other: This park also rents camping cottages, yurts, and modern cabins.
About the campground: Lakeside Campground, as the name implies, is closer to the water, which means you can roll out of bed in the morning and fish. But you might also have boaters within casting distance. Hillside Campground is more private but just a walk away from the lake and its recreational facilities.
Why it's worth a visit: This park gets a lot of visitors who might be termed "entry-level" outdoors people. As a result the park has placed a real emphasis on environmental programming. Here you can register for environmental education programs that cover a myriad of topics through traditional

classroom setting to recreation-based education platforms. The park even shows movies at the beach house and makes games available for loan at its beach area—anything to get children and families into the park, where they can be introduced to nature. There's plenty for the more experienced outdoors person too. The 78-acre lake gets stocked with trout several times a year and holds bass and panfish. There are also 9 miles of hiking trails to explore.

⑨ Raccoon Creek State Park

Location: West of Pittsburgh
Season: Second Fri in Apr to mid-Oct for the modern sites; year-round for the rustic Sioux Campground
Sites: 172, some ADA accessible
Maximum RV length: 40 feet
Facilities: Flush toilets, hot showers, water, electricity, sanitary dump station, picnic tables, fire rings, playground, boat launch
Fee per night: $$$–$$$$
Pets: Permitted at some sites
Activities: Swimming, boating, fishing, hunting, hiking, mountain biking, horseback riding, backpacking
Management: Pennsylvania Department of Conservation and Natural Resources
Contact: (724) 899-2200; www.dcnr.state.pa.us/stateparks/findapark/raccooncreek/index.htm. For reservations call toll-free (888) 727-2757 or visit VisitPaParks.com.
Finding the campground: From Pittsburgh follow I-376 (the Parkway) west for 10.6 miles. Get in the left lane as you cross the bridge to follow US 22/30 west. Follow US 22 west for 14.4 miles. Take the Route 18 north exit toward Florence, and turn left onto Route 18. Go 6 miles; turn left into the park and follow the signs.
GPS coordinates: N40 50.364'/W80 42.580'
Other: This park also rents modern cabins, a lodge, group cabins, and Adirondack shelters along a 19.5-mile backpacking trail. There's an organized group tenting area too.
About the campground: This large campground is made up of six loops. Five have their own shower houses, and two are open to pets.
Why it's worth a visit: The most distinctive thing at this park is its wildflower preserve. Its 314 acres house more than 700 species of plants, making it acre for acre one of the most diverse places in the commonwealth. The most flowers are in bloom late April and August, but there's always something to see. Call ahead to get a map and guide describing which species will be flowering by season. A side benefit of the reserve is that, because it's closed to all other activities but hiking, it holds lots of wildlife. Deer are common, as are squirrels and waterfowl. You can also usually see lots of wildlife, such as turkeys, near the campground and at some roadside picnic areas.

The park is also known for its active environmental education programming. The courses in primitive outdoors skills and winter camping are especially popular. The park's 101-acre lake offers opportunities to fish, boat, and swim. Its trails—including one that leads to Frankfort Mineral Springs, site of a popular resort in the 1830s—provide some wonderful hiking.

10 Ryerson Station State Park

Location: West of Waynesburg
Season: Year-round
Sites: 35, some ADA accessible
Maximum RV length: 40 feet
Facilities: Modern showers, vault toilets, sewer, water, electricity, sanitary dump station, picnic tables, fire rings
Fee per night: $$$–$$$$
Pets: Permitted at some sites
Activities: Swimming in a pool (free) that's open Memorial Day to Labor Day, fishing, hunting, hiking
Management: Pennsylvania Department of Conservation and Natural Resources
Contact: (724) 428-4254; www.dcnr.state.pa.us/stateparks/findapark/ryersonstation/index.htm. For reservations call toll-free (888) 727-2757 or visit VisitPaParks.com.
Finding the campground: From Waynesburg follow Routes 18/21 west until they split, then turn onto Route 21 west. Turn right onto Bristoria Road to enter the park. The campground will be on your left, on McNay Ridge Road.

Ryerson Station State Park's campground sits atop one of the region's many hills.

GPS coordinates: N39 88.384' / W80 44.885'

Other: When visiting this park, which also rents camping cottages and deluxe camping cottages and has an organized group tenting area, be sure to look for turkey vultures. As ugly as you'd expect up close, they are nonetheless beautiful in flight as they ride the air currents. The V shape of their giant wings differentiates them from hawks in flight.

About the campground: This small loop campground can be tight when full but is otherwise nice and sits atop one of the many rolling hills so common here. A 2019 renovation added modern showers, three deluxe camping cottages, full-service hookups on several sites, and a newly paved road.

Why it's worth a visit: The lake that used to be the hallmark of this park is now a field—dry save for the stream splitting it thanks to the dam having been breached for safety reasons. It's not coming back. State officials decided building a new reservoir just isn't feasible. But they are upgrading the parks in new ways, doing a stream restoration project, upgrading the pool, and more. And in the meantime, if you like peace and quiet, the lack of crowds can be refreshing. And there are still things to see and do here. Thirteen miles of hiking trails beg to be walked. One trail passes by Chess Cemetery, a graveyard deep in the woods, and beneath a cathedral of mature trees. Along the way you're likely to see white-tailed deer, gray and fox squirrels, and turkeys. Black bears, once unheard of in this part of the state, have started showing up here as well.

This is one of a handful of Pennsylvania campgrounds open year-round, so if you want to camp and hunt, snowshoe, or cross-country ski, this is a good option.

11 Youghiogheny River Lake Outflow Campground

Location: Just outside Confluence

Season: Year-round; no amenities from early Oct through early Apr

Sites: 64, some tent-only; some bike-and-hike sites that you have to walk or pedal to reach

Maximum RV length: 64 feet

Facilities: Flush toilets, warm showers, water, electricity, sanitary dump station, picnic tables, fire rings, boat launch

Fee per night: $$–$$$$; free camping without amenities during the off-season (Oct to early Apr)

Pets: Leashed pets permitted

Activities: Boating, waterskiing, tubing, swimming, biking (along Yough River Bike Trail), hiking, fishing, hunting

Management: US Army Corps of Engineers, Pittsburgh District

Contact: (814) 395-3242; www.lrp.usace.army.mil/missions/recreation/lakes/youghiogheny -river-lake/. For reservations call toll-free (877) 444-6777 or visit www.recreation.gov. There are limited first-come, first-served campsites in season; all sites are that way off-season.

Finding the campground: From Confluence go 0.5 mile south on Route 281; turn left at the campground sign.

GPS coordinates: N39 80.061' / W79 37.347'

Other: This is one of three campgrounds—one of them, Mill Run Campground, is actually in Maryland—offered at this lake.

About the campground: This campground offers many sites that are largely in the open. Hammock stations have been added to the hike-and-bike campsites. Alcoholic beverages are prohibited.

Why it's worth a visit: Youghiogheny River Lake is 16 miles long and up to 0.5 mile wide, so powerboaters absolutely love it. It's considered the best waterskiing and tubing lake in this half of the state, as the weekend crowds suggest. If there were such a thing as traffic lights for lakes, this one might need them, given its popularity.

There are lots of other things to do here though. The tailwater of the dam, located just outside your door or tent flap at this campground, is one of the few places open to year-round trout fishing. It's stocked by the state as well as by a local Trout Unlimited chapter, and there are some real beauties—fish in excess of 20 inches—to be caught. Some interesting wildlife can sometimes be glimpsed via a beautiful avenue. This is one of the first places in the state where otters were reintroduced, and they've thrived in the decades since. People who hike and bike along the Yough River's multiuse trail sometimes see them amid some especially beautiful scenery.

12 Youghiogheny River Lake Yough Lake Campground

Location: South of Confluence
Season: Apr to Oct
Sites: 101, some walk-in
Maximum RV length: 55 feet
Facilities: Flush toilets, warm showers, water, electricity, sanitary dump station, picnic tables, fire rings, boat launch
Fee per night: $$$–$$$$
Pets: Leashed pets permitted
Activities: Boating; canoe, kayak, and stand-up paddleboard rentals; waterskiing; tubing; swimming; biking (along Yough River Bike Trail); hiking; fishing; hunting
Management: US Army Corps of Engineers, Pittsburgh District
Contact: For information about the lake, contact the Army Corps at (814) 395-3242 or visit www .lrp.usace.army.mil/missions/recreation/lakes/youghiogheny-river-lake/. For information on the campground or for reservations contact Laurel Highlands River Tours and Outdoor Center at (800) 472-3846 or (724) 329-8531 or visit laurelhighlands.com/yough-lake-campground-tub-run/. There are limited first-come, first-served campsites.
Finding the campground: From Confluence follow Route 281 south until you can turn left onto Tub Run Road. Go 1 mile and follow the signs to the campground.
GPS coordinates: N39 76.764' / W79 39.922'
Other: Alcoholic beverages prohibited. There are some small rustic cabins for rent.
About the campground: Formerly known as Tub Run Campground and run by the Army Corps, the campground is now operated on a lease basis by a private concessionaire and is known as Yough Lake Campground. It is still the largest campground on the lake—a modern one at that, with its own boat launching ramp and swim beach for registered campers and their guests only.
Why it's worth a visit: This campground is a good base camp from which to explore some surrounding historical sites. Fallingwater and Kentuck Knob, two homes designed by renowned architect Frank Lloyd Wright, are just a short distance away, as are the Flight 93 Memorial and the Quecreek Mine Rescue Site. Fort Necessity, site of George Washington's defeat in the French and Indian War, is close by as well. The Western Pennsylvania Conservancy's nearly 5,600-acre Bear Run Nature Reserve—its flagship property—is just a short drive away and offers miles of hiking trails.

13 Ohiopyle State Park

Location: East of Uniontown
Season: Apr to mid-Dec
Sites: 209, 27 of them walk-in only and some ADA accessible
Maximum RV length: 40 feet
Facilities: Flush toilets, warm showers, water, electricity, sanitary dump station, picnic tables, fire rings
Fee per night: $$$-$$$$
Pets: Permitted at some sites
Activities: Natural waterslides, whitewater rafting, rock climbing, hiking, rail-trails, biking, mountain biking, horseback riding, fishing, hunting
Management: Pennsylvania Department of Conservation and Natural Resources
Contact: (724) 329-8591; www.dcnr.state.pa.us/stateparks/findapark/ohiopyle/index.htm. For reservations call toll-free (888) 727-2757 or visit VisitPaParks.com.

Cucumber Falls in Ohiopyle State Park runs heavy with springtime flows.

Finding the campground: From Uniontown follow US 40 east for 9 miles. Turn left (north) onto Route 381; go 6 miles and turn left again onto Kentuck Road. Go 1.5 miles; turn right onto Holland Hills Road and stay straight on Kentuck Trail to the campground.
GPS coordinates: N39 88.952' / W79 48.874'
Other: This park also rents camping cottages and yurts and has an organized group tenting area.
About the campground: This is a large campground, with lots of sites adjacent to trails. The walk-in sites near the Great Gorge Trail are nice.
Why it's worth a visit: Oh, where to start? This park has so many things going for it it's hard to decide what to do first. Many know Ohiopyle first and foremost for its whitewater rafting. The lower Youghiogheny (pronounced yawk-o-GAY-knee) River has some of the best, most consistent—and busiest—Class III and IV rafting in the Northeast, while the middle Youghiogheny is Class I and II water good for beginning whitewater enthusiasts. All of it can be tackled on your own or with the help of one of the many guide services located in town.

If riding the river is not your thing, the park has almost 80 miles of hiking trails. Some lead past waterfalls; others wind around Ferncliff Peninsula, site of an amusement park decades ago and today home to rare plants and fossils. You can fish for trout in the river or in one of its many tributary streams, bike 27 miles of the wonderfully scenic Great Allegheny Passage, put on your bathing suit and slide down natural waterslides, or take part in one of the park's many nature programs. Drive or climb to the Baughman Rocks overlook for a view of the deepest gorge in Pennsylvania. There are some designated horseback riding trails too.

14 Kooser State Park

Location: West of Somerset
Season: Mid-Apr through early Dec
Sites: 35, some ADA accessible
Maximum RV length: 40 feet
Facilities: Flush toilets, warm showers, water, electricity, coin-operated laundry, sanitary dump station, picnic tables, fire rings, lantern holders
Fee per night: $$$-$$$$
Pets: Permitted at all sites
Activities: Hiking, fishing
Management: Pennsylvania Department of Conservation and Natural Resources
Contact: (814) 445-8673; www.dcnr.state.pa.us/stateparks/findapark/kooser/index.htm. Reservations accepted by calling toll-free (888) 727-2757 or at VisitPaParks.com.
Finding the campground: From Somerset head west on Route 31 for about 10 miles. The entrance to the park and its campground is on the left.
GPS coordinates: N40 06.444' / W79 24.121'
Other: The park also has 9 rustic cabins available for rent.
About the campground: This is a small park by state standards, but the campground is anything but crowded. There's plenty of space between sites.
Why it's worth a visit: This park gets fewer visitors and fewer campers than nearby Laurel Hill State Park, likely because it's smaller in size with a smaller lake that offers no boating. But Kooser is a nice, quiet place to spend time. Kooser Run and the lake itself maintain cold temperatures

A young angler is all smiles after catching a bluegill at Kooser State Park's Kooser Lake.

year-round and hold trout for anglers. If you don't mind driving, you can stay here, drive 15 minutes to Laurel Hill for day activities, then come back to spend the night surrounded by fewer people.

Few day users of the park ever venture far from the lake, so the campground is very private. Be aware, though, that the park's swimming beach is closed permanently.

If you want to explore, the western edge of the park where the campground is located was where John Kooser, for whom the park is named, first settled in 1867. An Indian battle was later fought on the spot, and arrowheads and other artifacts have been found nearby.

15 Laurel Hill State Park

Location: West of Somerset
Season: Fri before opening day of trout season in mid-Apr to the third Sun in Oct
Sites: 264, some ADA accessible
Maximum RV length: 40 feet

Water tumbles over an old Civilian Conservation Corps dam on Jones Mill Run at Laurel Hill State Park.

Facilities: Flush toilets, hot showers, water, electricity, sanitary dump station, coin-operated laundry, picnic tables, fire rings

Fee per night: $$$-$$$$

Pets: Permitted at some sites

Activities: Environmental education programs, boating, swimming, hiking, fishing, hunting

Management: Pennsylvania Department of Conservation and Natural Resources

Contact: (814) 445-7725; www.dcnr.state.pa.us/stateparks/findapark/laurelhill/index.htm. For reservations call toll-free (888) 727-2757 or visit VisitPaParks.com.

Finding the campground: From Somerset go west on Route 31 for about 7 miles. Turn left onto Trent Road; go 1.7 miles and turn right at the sign into the park. Follow Park Road to the campground, on the right.

GPS coordinates: N39 99.071' / W79 24.179'

Other: This park also rents rustic cottages, a lodge, and one walled tent. It also has an organized group tenting area.

About the campground: This campground packs a lot of people into tight spaces, so don't expect loads of solitude. But the park is nice enough to make things worthwhile.

Why it's worth a visit: This is a very family-friendly park, meaning that it offers lots of options for those with children who might want to do multiple things in a day's time. It has a new swimming beach with playground equipment, a changing station, and a concession that gets lots of use.

There's a boat launch for those with their own crafts and boat rental for those who don't. Paddling the lake is very interesting. The shore opposite the beach is too steep to access from shore, so quietly floating along reveals things—perhaps scampering mink—shorebound folks never see. The lake and Laurel Hill Creek upstream and downstream of the dam offer fine trout fishing. The lake itself is open to trout fishing year-round, while the area upstream of the lake is open to those using artificial lures only.

The park has many miles of hiking trails as well. One not to be missed is the 1.6-mile Pumphouse Trail. This wide, mostly flat trail leads to Jones Mill Run Dam, a wonderfully scenic wall of cut stone built by men of the Civilian Conservation Corps in the 1930s.

Northern Pennsylvania

The Pennsylvania Wilds

Vegetation and driftwood mark the edges and surface of Black Moshannon Lake.

The Big Woods, the Northern Tier, or—in the more recent vernacular of tourism officials—the "Pennsylvania Wilds," this is the part of the state you come to if you're looking for big-time wilderness. It's home to more than 2.3 million acres of public land in the form of state parks and forests, state game lands, county parks, and the 500,000-plus-acre Allegheny, the state's only national forest.

It looks and feels the part. Other than I-80, the "highways" that bisect this region are few and far between and often only two lanes. Do a 9-mile float on the scenic Clarion River, for example, and it can take you 40 minutes of zigging and zagging to drive back to your starting point. Fast-food joints and shopping centers of any size are scarce and limited to the few sizable towns that qualify as anything more than a dot on the map. And gas stations? You're better off filling up early rather than late; it can be a while between fuel stops.

But that's the beauty of it all. This country is remote, often rugged, and always majestic.

Visit Cook Forest State Park and you'll find some of the most magnificent trees in this part of the world, such as the Longfellow Pine, which at more than 180 feet is the tallest of its kind in the Northeast. Allegheny National Forest offers miles upon miles of hiking; paddling along a federally designated Wild and Scenic River; ATV riding; backcountry grouse, black bear, and white-tailed deer hunting; and one of the nation's smallest federally protected wilderness area, the Allegheny Islands. This region is also where you come if you want to see a free-ranging herd of elk that boasts bulls big enough to qualify for the Boone & Crockett Club record book. You can bike through Pennsylvania's "Grand Canyon"—the trail's been called one of the ten best of its kind in the country—try hang gliding at Hyner View State Park, or stargaze at Cherry Springs State Park, the world's second international dark sky park.

When you're ready to come out of the woods for a while, you can tour factories such as the one where Zippo lighters and Case knives are made. You can visit the Pennsylvania Lumber Museum and Coalport Area Coal Museum, which pay tribute to the area's industrial heritage. You can learn about wildlife and conservation at the Elk Country Visitor Center or shop at the Woolrich factory store, where outdoor clothes and gear have been made since the 1830s. And you can enjoy road trips along Routes 120, 144, and 6—scenic byways that take you through little towns on the way to such attractions as the Kinzua Bridge Skywalk, a 301-foot-tall nineteenth-century railroad trestle you can walk across.

Whatever it is that brings you here, this region is a wonderful place to visit. No outdoor adventure in Pennsylvania is complete without stopping by.

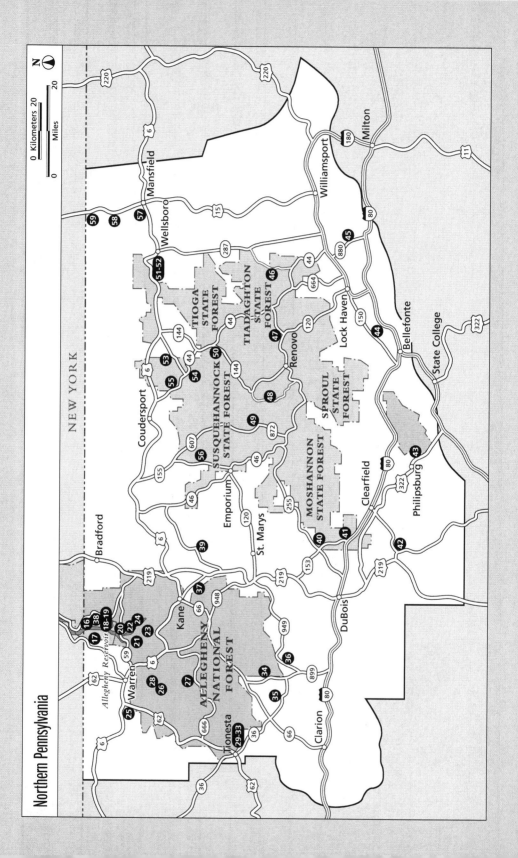

Park	Total Sites	Hookups	Max RV Length	Toilets	Showers	Drinking Water	Dump Station	Recreation	Fee	Reservation
16. Willow Bay Recreation Area	101	Y	60	F	Y	Y	Y	H, B, F, L, U	$$$–$$$$	Y
17. Hooks Brook Boat Access Campground	32	N/A	N/A	V	N	Y	N	B, F, S, U	$–$$	N
18. Handsome Lake Boat Access Campground	20	N/A	N/A	V	N	Y	N	H, B, F, U	$–$$	N
19. Hopewell Boat Access Campground	20	N/A	N/A	V	N	Y	N	H, B, F, S, U	$–$$	N
20. Pine Grove Boat Access Campground	13	N/A	N/A	V	N	Y	N	B, F, N	$–$$	N
21. Dewdrop Recreation Area	74	Y	50	F	Y	Y	Y	H, B, F, S, L, U	$$$–$$$$	Y
22. Morrison Boat Access Campground	38	N/A	N/A	V	N	Y	N	H, B, F, S, L, U	$–$$	N
23. Kiasutha Recreation Area	90	Y	45	F	Y	Y	Y	H, B, F, S, EE, U	$$$–$$$$	Y
24. Red Bridge Recreation Area	65	Y	60	F	Y	Y	Y	H, B, F, S, L, U	$$$–$$$$	Y
25. Buckaloons Recreation Area	61	Y	45	F	Y	Y	Y	H, B, F, L, U	$$$–$$$$	Y
26. Hearts Content Recreation Area	26	N	40	V	N	Y	Y	H, U	$$–$$$$	N
27. Minister Creek Campground	6	N	20	V	N	Y	N	H, F, U	$–$$	N
28. Chapman State Park	81	Y	60	F	Y	Y	Y	H, B, F, S, C, L, EE, U	$$$–$$$$	Y
29. Tionesta Lake Outflow Recreation Area	28	N	40	F	Y	Y	Y	H, B, F, C, L, U	$–$$	Y
30. Tionesta Lake Recreation Area	124	Y	75	F	Y	Y	Y	H, B, F, S, L, U	$$$$	Y
31. Tionesta Lake Lackey Flats Camping Area	17	N	N/A	V	N	Y	N	B, F, L	$	N
32. Tionesta Lake Glasner Run Camping Area	10	N	N/A	V	N	Y	N	F, B, L	$	N
33. Tionesta Lake Kellettville Recreation Area	20	N	60	F	N	Y	N	H, S, U	$–$$	N
34. Loleta Recreation Area	38	Y	50	F	Y	Y	N	H, F, S, U	$$$–$$$$	Y
35. Cook Forest State Park	205	Y	50	F	Y	Y	Y	H, B, F, C, L, R, EE, U	$$$–$$$$	Y
36. Clear Creek State Park	52	Y	40	F	Y	Y	Y	H, B, F, C, EE, U	$$$–$$$$	Y
37. Twin Lakes Recreation Area	48	Y	28	F	Y	Y	Y	H, F, U	$$–$$$$	Y
38. Tracy Ridge Recreation Area	119	N	50	V	N	Y	Y	H, U	$–$$	Y

Park	Total Sites	Hookups	Max RV Length	Toilets	Showers	Drinking water	Dump station	Recreation	Fee	Reservation
39. Elk State Park	41	Y	70	F	Y	Y	Y	H, B, F, C, U	$$$–$$$$	N
40. Parker Dam State Park	109	Y	40	F	Y	Y	Y	H, B, F, S, L, EE, U	$$$–$$$$	Y
41. Simon B. Elliott State Park	25	N	40	F	N	Y	Y	H, F, U	$$–$$$$	Y
42. Curwensville Lake	51	Y	60	F	Y	Y	N	H, B, F, S, C, L	$$$–$$$$	Y
43. Black Moshannon State Park	73	Y	40	F	Y	Y	Y	H, B, F, S, C, L, EE, U	$$$–$$$$	Y
44. Bald Eagle State Park	160	Y	40	F	Y	Y	Y	H, B, F, S, L, EE, U	$$$–$$$$	Y
45. Ravensburg State Park	21	N	N/A	V	Y	Y	N	H, F	$$–$$$$	N
46. Little Pine State Park	99	Y	50	F	Y	Y	Y	H, B, F, S, L, EE, U	$$$–$$$$	Y
47. Hyner Run State Park	30	Y	56	F	Y	Y	Y	H, F, EE, U	$$$–$$$$	Y
48. Kettle Creek State Park	68	Y	45	F	Y	Y	Y	H, B, F, C, L, EE, U	$$$–$$$$	Y
49. Sinnemahoning State Park	35	Y	75	F	Y	Y	Y	H, B, F, C, EE, U	$$$–$$$$	Y
50. Ole Bull State Park	77	Y	40	F	Y	Y	Y	H, F, S, EE, U	$$$–$$$$	Y
51. Leonard Harrison State Park	25	Y	100	F	Y	Y	Y	H, F, EE, U	$$$–$$$$	Y
52. Colton Point State Park	21	N	30	V	N	N	N	H, B, F, EE, U	$$–$$$$	N
53. Lyman Run State Park	35	Y	134	F	Y	Y	Y	H, B, F, S, L, EE, U, O	$$$–$$$$	Y
54. Cherry Springs State Park	30	N	81	V	N	Y	Y	H, C, EE, U	$$–$$$$	N
55. Patterson State Park	10	N	40	V	N	Y	N	H, C, U	$$–$$$$	N
56. Sizerville State Park	23	Y	40	F	Y	Y	Y	H, F, S, U	$$$–$$$$	Y
57. Hills Creek State Park	80	Y	96	F	Y	Y	Y	H, B, F, S, L, EE, U	$$$–$$$$	Y
58. Tioga–Hammond Lakes Ives Run Campground	150	Y	100	F	Y	Y	Y	H, B, F, S, L, U	$$$–$$$$	Y
59. Cowanesque Lake Tompkins Campground	86	Y	68	F	Y	Y	Y	H, B, F, S, L, U	$$$–$$$$	Y

Y = yes, N = no
Toilets: F = flush, V = vault
Recreation: H = hiking, B = boating, F = fishing, S = swimming, C = cycling, L = boat launch, R = horseback riding, EE = environmental education, U = hunting; O = off-road vehicle area.
Fee: $ to $$$$

16 Willow Bay Recreation Area

Location: West of Bradford
Season: Year-round; best access from about Apr 1 to Oct 20 (no winter maintenance)
Sites: 101, some ADA accessible and some walk-in only
Maximum length: 60 feet
Facilities: Flush and rustic toilets, warm showers, water, electricity, sanitary dump station, picnic tables, fire rings, grills, boat launch, boat rental
Fee per night: $$$-$$$$
Pets: Leashed pets permitted
Activities: Boating, hiking, fishing, hunting
Management: Allegheny National Forest
Contact: (814) 723-5150; www.fs.usda.gov/allegheny/. For reservations call (814) 444-6777 or visit www.recreation.gov. Reservations during the off-season (between Labor Day and Memorial Day weekends) can be made by calling (814) 368-4158.
Finding the campground: From Bradford go west on Route 346 to the campground, which is located just south of the New York state line.

A great spangled fritillary alights on a wildflower at Willow Bay Recreation Area.

GPS coordinates: N41 98.778' / W78 91.056'

Other: There are also cabins available for rent.

About the campground: The sites in Deer Grove Camping Area and Hemlock Loop overlook the south shore of Willow Bay; those in Aspen Loop parallel Willow Creek. Some are in the open and unlike anything else in the Allegheny; others are in the shade of mature hemlocks.

Why it's worth a visit: Built in the 1960s, and so decades newer than some other state facilities, this campground was recently renovated. It offers the opportunity to do all the usual things—hike, fish, and picnic—but you can also rent boats, from fishing and pleasure boats to pontoons. The hiking can be especially good, as the North Country National Scenic Trail passes by here. And there's some neat history to explore.

The Seneca-Iroquois Indian Museum and the Salamanca Rail Museum are located just 30 minutes over the state line in Salamanca, New York. The Riverview-Corydon Cemetery, which was created in the early 1800s and is a historic Native American grave site, is less than 3 miles north-west of Willow Bay.

17 Hooks Brook Boat Access Campground

Location: Northeast of Warren

Season: Apr 1 to Dec 15; best access until Oct 20 (no winter maintenance)

Sites: 32

Maximum RV length: N/A

Facilities: Vault toilets, water, picnic tables, fire rings

Fee per night: $–$$

Pets: Leashed pets permitted

Activities: Boating, waterskiing, windsurfing, tubing, swimming, hunting, fishing

Management: Allegheny National Forest

Contact: (814) 723-5150; www.fs.usda.gov/allegheny/. No reservations accepted; it's first come, first served.

Finding the campground: The closest boat launches are at Webbs Ferry, about 1 mile to the north on the west bank, and at Willow Bay, also about 1 mile north but on the east bank.

GPS coordinates: N41 96.223' / W78 94.243'

Other: Senior and Access passes, available through any of the forest offices, entitle visitors to a 50 percent discount on these and other campsites.

About the campground: This campground has the benefit of being fairly secluded, without good foot access, so it's lightly used and popular with those who like solitude.

Why it's worth a visit: A lot of wildlife calls Allegheny National Forest home—black bears, white-tailed deer, bobcats, coyotes, squirrels, raccoons, birds of all manner and variety—and sometimes being in a boat increases your chances of spotting it. Maybe we seem less threatening when we're on the water; maybe it's that we move more quietly. Whatever the case, floating gets you close to wildlife, and camping here puts you in the midst of all those animals. Keep an eye open for some-times spectacular critters, including bald eagles. There are sufficient numbers living on and around the reservoir that official eagle watches are held at various sites around the reservoir each winter. Chances are you might spot an eagle on your trip here.

Be sure to keep your food packed away—no sense tempting anything to share your meals.

18 Handsome Lake Boat Access Campground

Location: Northwest of Marshburg
Season: Year-round
Sites: 20
Maximum RV length: N/A
Facilities: Vault toilets, water in season (pack it in on the edges of the year), picnic tables, fire rings, grills
Fee per night: $-$$
Pets: Leashed pets permitted
Activities: Boating, waterskiing, windsurfing, tubing, swimming, hiking, fishing, hunting
Management: Allegheny National Forest
Contact: (814) 723-5150; www.fs.usda.gov/allegheny/. No reservations accepted; it's first come, first served.
Finding the campground: The closest boat launches are at Roper Hollow, directly across the reservoir on the west bank, and at Kinzua Wolf Run Marina, about 5 miles south near Route 59 at the Morrison Bridge.
GPS coordinates: N41 92.278'/W78 93.222'
Other: This campsite is accessible by foot or boat only. Hike-in access is via the North Country National Scenic Trail, with connections to the Tracy Ridge Trail System.
About the campground: It's located on the east bank of Allegheny Reservoir, just north of Sugar Bay.
Why it's worth a visit: Boat-in accesses like this one are by their nature primitive and secluded. There are no boat docks—nothing more obvious in terms of human habitation than picnic tables— so they don't attract a lot of attention from casual boaters. Only a relative handful of hikers make it this far in either. That means this site, and others like it, offer the opportunity to do some backcountry camping. The difference is that, unlike with backpacking, your boat allows you to carry in enough gear to make yourself comfortable.

You want to make the most of the opportunity, so remember a few things: Make a packing list before you go so that you don't leave any essential gear behind. Store your supplies onshore and off the boat when you arrive to keep them dry and handy. Bring a camera and keep it accessible so that you don't miss out on photo opportunities. Most important, leave a float plan with someone responsible; note when you're leaving, who's going with you, and when you expect to be back. If you don't show up when expected, rescuers will know where to start searching for you.

19 Hopewell Boat Access Campground

Location: Northwest of Marshburg
Season: Year-round; best access Apr 1 to Oct 20 (no winter maintenance)
Sites: 20
Maximum RV length: N/A
Facilities: Vault toilets, water, picnic tables, fire rings
Fee per night: $-$$

Pets: Leashed pets permitted

Activities: Boating, swimming, waterskiing, windsurfing, tubing, hiking, fishing, hunting

Management: Allegheny National Forest

Contact: (814) 723-5150; www.fs.usda.gov/allegheny/. No reservations accepted; it's first come, first served.

Finding the campground: The closest boat launches are at Roper Hollow, directly across the reservoir on the west bank, and at Kinzua Wolf Run Marina, about 5 miles south near Route 59 at the Morrison Bridge.

GPS coordinates: N41 91.957' / W78 93.346'

Other: This campsite is accessible by foot or boat only. Hike-in access is via the North Country National Scenic Trail, with connections to the Tracy Ridge Trail System.

About the campground: It's located on the east bank of Allegheny Reservoir, just north of Sugar Bay. It's located just south of Hammond Lake Boat Access Campground.

Why it's worth a visit: This campground can be accessed on foot, it's true. But it's not at all easy. If you walk in here, you will find yourself climbing in and out of valleys, experiencing frequent and noticeably difficult elevation changes along the way. Once you're in, it's still hard to get right on the water given the steep, rocky hillsides. Suffice it to say that if you boat in, you won't often have a lot of competition for campsites. You might spot some interesting and largely undisturbed wildlife though. Just be sure to take along a weather radio. A little warning about approaching storms gives you the opportunity to prepare your boat and campsite for rough patches.

20 Pine Grove Boat Access Campground

Location: East of Warren

Season: Year-round; best access through Oct 20 (no winter maintenance)

Sites: 13

Maximum RV length: N/A

Facilities: Vault toilets, pump water, picnic tables, fire rings

Fee per night: $–$$

Pets: Leashed pets permitted

Activities: Boating, waterskiing, tubing, fishing, hunting

Management: Allegheny National Forest

Contact: (814) 723-5150; www.fs.usda.gov/allegheny/. No reservations accepted; it's first come, first served.

Finding the campground: The closest boat launch is at Kinzua Wolf Run Marina, about 1 mile south near Route 59 at the Morrison Bridge.

GPS coordinates: N41 87.592' / W78 94.638'

Other: There are no boat docks here. It's recommended that you pack in your own water during the off-season.

About the campground: This small rustic campground is located on the east bank of the Allegheny Reservoir just north of Kinzua Wolf Run Marina. It is accessible only by boat.

Why it's worth a visit: With no hiking trails leading to this campground, no boat docks, and no boat launches closer than 1 mile away, and located as it is on one of the widest spots on Allegheny Reservoir, this is the place to go to rough it. Not many do; usage of this campground is admittedly light, especially on weekdays. But that's the attraction. Watch the sun set over the steep hillsides and the water, and you'll understand why it's worth the effort to set up here.

Be aware that the same factors that make it difficult to get to this camp make it hard to get out. Give your boat a thorough check before you head out, and carry extra gas and a few tools in case you experience problems on the water. A radio that you can use to call for help is good equipment to have along too.

21 Dewdrop Recreation Area

Location: East of Warren
Season: Memorial Day weekend through Labor Day weekend
Sites: 74, some ADA accessible and some walk-in only
Maximum RV length: 50 feet
Facilities: Flush toilets, warm showers, water, electricity, sanitary dump station, picnic tables, fire ring or grill, parking for two vehicles and a wheeled camping unit, boat launch
Fee per night: $$$-$$$$

Powerboating is very popular on Allegheny Reservoir at Dewdrop Recreation Area in Allegheny National Forest.

Pets: Leashed pets permitted

Activities: Boating, swimming, hiking, scenic drives, fishing, hunting

Management: Allegheny National Forest

Contact: (814) 723-5150; www.fs.usda.gov/allegheny/. For reservations call (814) 444-6777 or visit www.recreation.gov.

Finding the campground: From Warren take Route 59 east for 13 miles. Turn onto Longhouse Scenic Byway/FR 262 south; continue 3 miles to the campground.

GPS coordinates: N41 83.194' / W78 95.944'

Other: This is a good base from which to do some scenic driving. A variety of planned routes are available, some sticking completely to paved roads, others using dirt forest service roads. Maps can be purchased at any forest service office.

About the campground: This campground is a series of loops and offers the chance to be right on the lakeshore or farther away.

Why it's worth a visit: This campground sits on the Kinzua Arm of Allegheny Reservoir, just south of Kinzua Point. The lake is wider and deeper here, so the location and its launch facilities make it ideal for campers who want to be able to hit the water to fish, ski, tube, or just relax.

And use it people do. Visit this area on a sunny summer weekend and you'll find motorboats and personal watercraft crisscrossing the lake, pulling skiers and tubers and making waves. The nearby Elijah Launch allows noncampers to get on the water too, so things will be busy. That lends itself to a bit of a party atmosphere, and camaraderie is a big part of the attraction here. When you come off the lake and want to take a hike, a relatively easy 2.5-mile interpretive trail winds around the campground.

22 Morrison Boat Access Campground

Location: Southwest of Marshburg

Season: Apr 1 to Dec 15; best access through Oct 20 (no winter maintenance)

Sites: 38

Maximum RV length: N/A

Facilities: Vault toilets, water in season (pack it in on the edges of the year), picnic tables, fire rings

Fee per night: $-$$

Pets: Leashed pets permitted

Activities: Boating, waterskiing, tubing, windsurfing, swimming, hiking, fishing, hunting

Management: Allegheny National Forest

Contact: (814) 723-5150; www.fs.usda.gov/allegheny/. No reservations accepted; it's first come, first served.

Finding the campground: The closest boat launches are at Elijah Run, directly west of the campground, or at Kinzua Wolf Run Marina, about 3 miles north near the Morrison Bridge at Route 59.

GPS coordinates: N41 82.062' / W78 92.793'

Other: Mid- to late June, when the mountain laurel is in full bloom, is a nice time to visit this campground.

About the campground: This campground is located on the east bank of Kinzua Bay, immediately west of Elijah Run Boat Launch. It's accessible only by boat or by hiking in via the Morrison Hiking Trail.

Why it's worth a visit: This is one of the boat-to campgrounds that actually gets a few hikers. Morrison Trail is an 11.4-mile loop that makes for an easy overnight backpacking trip, so more than a few folks pack their way in. Still, as at Hopewell Boat Access Campground and most of the others like it around Allegheny Reservoir, this campground features steep hillsides, so while hikers can get here, it's tough for them to access most of the shoreline.

Boaters can enjoy the best of two worlds: You can motor in and out, fish and ski and do your thing on the water, and then set up camp and venture into the second-growth forests of oak, hickory, white pines, and, along the stream edges, hemlock. If you plan to take a walk in the woods, remember to pack hiking shoes. The sandals or flip-flops you wear on the boat won't cut it on the trail.

23 Kiasutha Recreation Area

Location: Northwest of Kane
Season: Memorial Day weekend through Labor Day weekend
Sites: 90, some ADA accessible
Maximum RV length: 45 feet
Facilities: Flush toilets, warm showers, water, electricity, sanitary dump station, picnic tables, fire rings, playground, amphitheater, seasonal camp store
Fee per night: $$$-$$$$
Pets: Leashed pets permitted
Activities: Boating, swimming, environmental education programs, hiking, fishing, hunting
Management: Allegheny National Forest
Contact: (814) 723-5150; www.fs.usda.gov/allegheny/. For reservations call (814) 444-6777 or visit www.recreation.gov. First-come, first-served sites are also available.
Finding the campground: From Kane take Route 321 north for 10 miles. Turn left onto Longhouse Scenic Drive and continue for 1 mile to the campground.
GPS coordinates: N41 78.315' / W78 89.909'
Other: The large grassy beach in the day-use area, with a capacity of 900 people, is especially popular with families. There's a bathhouse there too.
About the campground: This campground is a series of loops. Some of its nonelectric sites, mainly those on the outer edges of the loops, afford the most privacy.
Why it's worth a visit: This is a very large recreation area, and its day-use facilities draw a lot more people than just campers. People come to swim, to play games on the large grassy opening, and to fish. Spending the weekend won't be an exercise in solitary confinement, but there's plenty to do. There are no "official" hiking trails, but anglers and others have created some pretty identifiable footpaths along the water's edge and through the woods that you can explore. The requisite boat launch—every spot on the Allegheny Reservoir seems to have one—means you can use this campground as a base for time spent on the water.

The recreation area is located so that you can choose the pace at which you want to have your fun. Head north toward the Morrison and Dewdrop Campgrounds and you can mix it up with the skiers and tubers; head south toward Red Bridge campground and you'll be in shallower, quieter water perfect for fishing.

24 Red Bridge Recreation Area

Location: Northwest of Kane
Season: Apr 15 to Oct 31
Sites: 65, some ADA accessible and some walk-in only
Maximum RV length: 60 feet
Facilities: Flush toilets, warm showers, water, electricity, sanitary dump station, picnic tables, fire rings, playground, seasonal camp store, boat launch suitable for small craft
Fee per night: $$$–$$$$
Pets: Leashed pets permitted

A tent lies partially hidden by foliage in the walk-in section of the Red Bridge Recreation Area campground in Allegheny National Forest.

Activities: Boating, swimming, hiking, fishing, hunting

Management: Allegheny National Forest

Contact: (814) 723-5150; www.fs.usda.gov/allegheny/. For reservations call (814) 444-6777 or visit www.recreation.gov. Some first-come, first-served sites are also available.

Finding the campground: From Kane head north on Route 321 until you reach the campground, on your right.

GPS coordinates: N41 77.669'/W78 88.630'

Other: This campground has a bank fishing area where it's easy to access the water. As you drive or walk to its parking area, you'll notice a marker memorializing this spot as a place where German prisoners of war were held temporarily during World War II. Ospreys, large birds of prey that feast on fish, maintain a nest in this area, so be sure to look for them.

About the campground: This campground is heavily wooded with mature cherry, hemlock, and birch trees. Some sites are on the waterfront; others offer views of the water.

Why it's worth a visit: This is an all-around sort of campground. What does that mean? Some campgrounds are desirable because they're especially small or remote, cater to big boats, or are adjacent to some particularly fascinating natural feature. Then there are those like Red Bridge. Its charm—and the reason it's always busy—is that it offers a little bit of everything. You can fish, hike, play, enjoy a campfire, and swim, all in the same day in the same place. That makes it perfect if you've got kids who want to do this, then that, throughout the day.

The feel here is relaxed rather than frenetic though. The lake is plied not by powerboats but by canoes, kayaks, and smaller fishing boats. Families walk the quiet campground, and anglers set up chairs along the shore to fish. The hiking comes in the form of the North Country National Scenic Trail, which crosses Route 321 just 0.25 mile south of the campground.

25 Buckaloons Recreation Area

Location: West of Warren

Season: May to late Oct

Sites: 61

Maximum RV length: 45 feet

Facilities: Flush toilets, warm showers, water, electricity, sanitary dump station, picnic table, fire ring or grill, boat launch, playground, parking for two vehicles and a wheeled camping unit

Fee per night: $$$–$$$$

Pets: Leashed pets permitted

Activities: Hiking, fishing, hunting, boating, kayaking

Management: Allegheny National Forest

Contact: (814) 723-5150; www.fs.usda.gov/allegheny/. For reservations call (814) 444-6777 or visit www.recreation.gov.

Finding the campground: From Warren go 6.5 miles west on US 6. Turn left onto US 62 south, then make the first right into the recreation area.

GPS coordinates: N41 83.972'/W79 25.639'

Other: This area was once the site of a Native American trading post and is considered northwestern Pennsylvania's richest archaeological site. Artifacts dating back 12,000 years have been discovered here.

About the campground: This campground offers two double sites as well as an organized group tenting area. Drivers should be aware of low branches and power lines, especially at parking aprons.

Why it's worth a visit: Situated where Brokenstraw Creek and Irvine Run empty into the Allegheny River, this campground is surrounded by lots of wildlife that often can be seen by walking the Seneca Interpretive Trail, with its abundance of apple trees. What really draws people to this campground though is that it's a wonderful launch spot for some paddling. The Allegheny is a Class I river that offers dependable flows year-round, so many people come here to camp and float in their canoe or kayak. You can put in just below Kinzua Dam near Warren and float to the campground, spend the night, then continue'on down to any one of several launches for a nice two-day float.

Just a few miles downstream of the campground is the Allegheny Islands Wilderness Area—a collection of seven islands that, at less than 400 acres total, represents one of the smallest federally protected wilderness area in the country. The islands are fun to explore and even camp on and are home to some spectacular woods. The national champion dotted hawthorn was recently discovered on one of the islands, as were a 147-foot-tall sycamore and multitrunk silver maples with trunks more than 25 feet around.

A number of outfitters operate in the area in case you need to rent a boat. Just be sure to bring your fishing rod: The fishing can be exceptional, with trophy trout, smallmouth bass, muskies, and walleyes all there for the catching.

26 Hearts Content Recreation Area

Location: Southwest of Warren
Season: May 1 to Oct 24; best access until Oct 20 (no winter maintenance)
Sites: 26
Maximum RV length: 40 feet
Facilities: Rustic toilets, water, sanitary dump station, picnic tables, fire rings, grills at the lean-tos, playground
Fee per night: $$–$$$
Pets: Leashed pets permitted
Activities: Hiking, orienteering, hunting
Management: Allegheny National Forest
Contact: (814) 723-5150; www.fs.usda.gov/allegheny/. No reservations accepted; it's first come, first served.
Finding the campground: From US 6 near Warren, take Route 3005/Pleasant Drive south for 11 miles. At the hard curve, turn left onto Route 2002, a gravel road, and go south for 4 miles to the campground.
GPS coordinates: N41 69.033' / W79 25.537'
Other: Organized group tenting area; 2 lean-to shelters with charcoal grills
About the campground: Civilian Conservation Corps workers constructed the campground, picnic area, and pavilion here in 1936. An exhibit of a hand-hewed log is adjacent to the picnic area.

Why it's worth a visit: This campground is the place to be if you're into hiking. You can access Old Growth Trail, a 1.1-mile interpretive walk that goes through Hearts Content Scenic Area—a 200-plus-acre virgin forest of 300- to 400-year-old trees. When you realize that some of the massive trees standing here, their bark deeply furrowed like worry lines on a giant's face, were already old when George Washington was born, that's pretty awe-inspiring.

Take the time to really look at the trees. Their trunks attach to the ground like dinosaur toes. Others that have crashed to the ground are covered in moss—evidence of nature's recycling—or lie bare, their broken limbs looking like the antlers of a fallen stag. As you walk, listen for the chipmunks that are constantly squeaking and scampering about.

There's also a 6.4-mile cross-country ski trail. And if you want to get more adventurous, the 8,663-acre Hickory Creek Wilderness surrounds the campground and offers some wonderful opportunities to explore where only foot travel is permitted. The trailhead—which was supposed to be moved away from the parking lot as of this writing—will still be located somewhere in this area and is the launch point for an 11-mile loop trail.

27 Minister Creek Campground

Location: Southwest of Sheffield
Season: Year-round; best access Apr 1 to Oct 20 (no winter maintenance)
Sites: 6
Maximum length: 20 feet
Facilities: Vault toilets, water, picnic table, fire ring
Fee per night: $-$$
Pets: Leashed pets permitted
Activities: Hiking, fishing, hunting
Management: Allegheny National Forest
Contact: (814) 723-5150; www.fs.usda.gov/allegheny/. No reservations accepted; it's first come, first served.
Finding the campground: From Sheffield follow Route 666 south for 14.7 miles to the campground, on your right.
GPS coordinates: N41 62.070'/W79 15.426'
Other: If you want to explore this area or fish Minister Creek without camping, you can park in a gravel lot directly across Route 666 from the campground entrance.
About the campground: This is a tiny one, with just a half-dozen sites, and it's right along the road's edge. It's beautiful nonetheless, with babbling Minister Creek right outside your tent or RV window.
Why it's worth a visit: There are a lot of reasons to like this campground. If you canoe or kayak, the trip along Tionesta Creek from Sheffield to Minister Creek is a lovely one, though it's best done in spring before Tionesta Creek gets too low. If it's hiking you prefer, the 6-mile Minister Creek Trail loop is a dandy that connects to the North Country National Scenic Trail.

The campground is also a perfect jumping-off spot if you like to fish small streams for native brook trout. Minister Creek is home to a good population of fish that swim beneath hemlocks and

Allegheny National Forest's Minister Creek Campground is small but scenic and sits right next to a stream that holds native brook trout.

big woods. Catch one and you'll see why it's special. The fish won't necessarily be big—an 8-incher might be a whopper—but brook trout are electrically colorful.

28 Chapman State Park

Location: South of Warren
Season: Mid-Apr to mid-Dec
Sites: 81, some ADA accessible and some walk-in only
Maximum RV length: 60 feet
Facilities: Flush toilets, showers, water, electricity, sanitary dump station, picnic tables, fire rings, swimming beach, concession stand, boat launches (unpowered and electric motors only), boat rental, hiking and mountain biking trails, environmental education programs
Fee per night: $$$–$$$$
Pets: Permitted at sites 1–43

Activities: Boating, swimming, hiking, mountain biking, fishing, hunting

Management: Pennsylvania Department of Conservation and Natural Resources

Contact: (814) 723-0250; www.dcnr.state.pa.us/stateparks/findapark/chapman/index.htm. For reservations call toll-free (888) 727-2757 or visit VisitPaParks.com.

Finding the campground: From Warren follow US 6 east for about 6 miles. Turn on to Railroad Street in the town of Clarendon, which becomes Chapman Dam Road. Follow Chapman Dam Road 5 miles to the park.

GPS coordinates: N41 74.661' / W79 17.469'

Other: This park has 3 cottages and 2 yurts for rent and an organized group tenting area.

About the campground: If you're looking for a little more privacy without having to backpack, this campground offers a dozen walk-in sites that are just far enough away from the road to lose your neighbors. All are adjacent to the nature trail.

Why it's worth a visit: This is a relatively small park with a big feel. It's 862 acres but is situated next to the 500,000-plus-acre Allegheny National Forest and some other public ground, so it's a bit of a tucked-away gem. It's also another site that's great for families and children.

The relatively large sandy beach is clean and pretty, and a large concession stand on the edge will help you keep the kids fed. There are grassy areas for playing games, a playground, and, adjacent to the beach, a boat rental where you can rent a canoe or kayak. There's a fishing pier nearby and lots of shore access, so you can do a lot of exploring too.

A variety of environmental education programs are held in summer, ranging from bike parades for children to hikes, stargazing sessions, and wildlife talks. Later in the year this park is popular with hunters, who stay here and do their thing in parts of the park and nearby public lands.

29 Tionesta Lake Outflow Recreation Area

Location: South of Tionesta

Season: Year-round

Sites: 28, some ADA accessible

Maximum RV length: 40 feet

Facilities: Flush toilets, warm showers, water, sanitary dump station (mid-Apr to mid-Oct only); picnic tables, fire rings, playground, boat launch

Fee per night: $–$$ (mid-Apr to late Oct)

Pets: Leashed pets permitted

Activities: Boating, waterskiing, tubing, swimming, hiking, biking, fishing, hunting

Management: US Army Corps of Engineers, Pittsburgh District

Contact: (814) 755-3512; www.lrp.usace.army.mil/missions/recreation/lakes/tionesta-lake/. For reservations call toll-free (877) 444-6777 or visit recreation.gov.

Finding the campground: From Tionesta go 0.5 mile south on Route 36 and follow signs into the campground

GPS coordinates: N41 48.472' / W79 44.861'

Other: This area, all forested today, was logged in the early twentieth century, when narrow-gauge railroads hauled out virgin timber. Camping is offered on a free, first-come, first-served basis from after Labor Day through the weekend before Memorial Day.

About the campground: While this campground on the northern side of Tionesta Lake can handle RVs, some of its sites are more suited to tents, as the camping spurs are not well defined. Alcohol is prohibited.

Why it's worth a visit: This campground is a good option if you are looking for a little more quiet. Its lack of facilities relative to some other nearby campgrounds means it draws smaller crowds of primarily tent campers. It's also especially nice if you plan to visit in the fall. The opportunity to hike, bike, or hunt in these woods when they're ablaze in oranges, reds, and yellows is very special. Another benefit is that you can sometimes camp here for free. The campground is open year-round, but fees are only charged from mid-April through October. If you come here in late fall or winter—to hunt, get in some ice fishing, or ski or snowshoe—there's no cost. Of course there are no amenities either.

30 Tionesta Lake Recreation Area

Location: South of Tionesta
Season: mid-May to Sept
Sites: 124
Maximum length: 75 feet
Facilities: Flush toilets, warm showers, water, electricity, sanitary dump station, picnic tables, fire rings, boat launches, playground
Fee per night: $$$$
Pets: Leashed pets permitted
Activities: Boating, waterskiing, tubing, swimming, hiking, biking, fishing, hunting
Management: US Army Corps of Engineers, Pittsburgh District
Contact: (814) 755-3512; www.lrp.usace.army.mil/missions/recreation/lakes/tionesta-lake/. For reservations call toll-free (877) 444-6777 or visit www.recreation.gov. There are some first-come, first-served campsites too.
Finding the campground: From Tionesta go 0.5 mile south on Route 36 and follow the signs into the campground
GPS coordinates: N41 48.472' / W79 44.861'
Other: The Seneca Indians named this area "where the water separates the land," presumably because of its many creeks and rivers.
About the campground: This campground was recently renovated and is by far the largest and most modern of those at Tionesta. The sites are densely congregated, so you won't find much in the way of privacy. Alcoholic beverages are prohibited.
Why it's worth a visit: Tionesta Lake, which covers 480 acres at normal summer pool, is the main draw. A large body of water in a remote, mountainous setting, it's great for boating and fishing. That doesn't apply to just larger boats either. As with all the campgrounds at this facility, a nice option in spring when there's sufficient water and flow is to canoe or kayak Tionesta Creek from Kellettville or even farther upstream at Sheffield down to the main lake. There is a locally famous bridge at the Nebraska Recreation Area that has to be portaged though, so be prepared for that. A public beach is located just downstream of the campground, and there are a couple of hiking trails worth exploring: the Mill Race Trail, which connects the ends of the campground, and the Dam Site Trail.

Raindrops pool on a leaf near the Outflow Recreation Area at Tionesta Lake.

31 Tionesta Lake Lackey Flats Camping Area

Location: East of Tionesta
Season: Year-round, weather permitting
Sites: 17, all boat-in only
Maximum length: N/A
Facilities: Water and restrooms available at the boat launch ramp, fire rings
Fee per night: $ to launch your boat; no fee to camp
Pets: Leashed pets permitted
Activities: Boating, fishing, hunting
Management: US Army Corps of Engineers, Pittsburgh District
Contact: (814) 755-3512; www.lrp.usace.army.mil/missions/recreation/lakes/tionesta-lake/. No reservations accepted; it's first come, first served.
Finding the campground: Access the campground from the public boat launching ramp at Tionesta Lake.
GPS coordinates: N41 48.472' / W79 44.861'
Other: Alcoholic beverages are prohibited.
About the campground: Campsites are designated with a numbered post and a fire ring.
Why it's worth a visit: Lackey Flats is on the southern shore of Tionesta Lake, about 2 miles upstream of the launching ramp at Tionesta Recreation Area. It's a boat-in only site, but it can be fairly busy on weekends.

One thing to keep in mind is that the Pittsburgh District of the Corps requires children younger than 13 to wear a life jacket at all times when on this lake. If you don't have enough life jackets, this is a "life jacket loaner program" site, with about fifteen life jackets in three sizes for children: infant, child, and youth. Boaters can sign out life jackets and return them at the end of their excursion. Most borrowers keep them for only a day, but details are available by calling the Corps office.

32 Tionesta Lake Glasner Run Camping Area

Location: East of Tionesta
Season: Year-round, weather permitting
Sites: 10, all boat-in only
Maximum length: N/A
Facilities: Water and restrooms available at the boat launch ramp, fire rings
Fee per night: $ to launch your boat; no fee to camp
Pets: Leashed pets permitted
Activities: Boating, fishing, hunting
Management: US Army Corps of Engineers, Pittsburgh District
Contact: (814) 755-3512; www.lrp.usace.army.mil/missions/recreation/lakes/tionesta-lake/. No reservations accepted; it's first come, first served.
Finding the campground: Access the campground from the public boat launching ramp at Tionesta Lake.
GPS coordinates: N41 48.472' / W79 44.861'

Other: Alcoholic beverages are prohibited.

About the campground: Campsites are designated with a numbered post and a fire ring.

Why it's worth a visit: This campground is located on the northern shore of Tionesta Lake, about 1 mile upstream of the launching ramp at Tionesta Recreation Area, and is much like the one at Lackey Flats in that it offers primitive lakeside camping. If you find this site full, as can happen on holiday weekends, there are nineteen additional campsites on adjacent forest service land. Otherwise this is especially worth visiting during low-competition weekday periods.

33 Tionesta Lake Kellettville Recreation Area

Location: East of Tionesta

Season: May to Sept (at the time of this writing, keeping the campground open through Oct was being considered)

Sites: 20, some ADA accessible

Maximum length: 60 feet

Facilities: Flush toilets and water, picnic tables, fire rings, playground

Fee per night: $-$$ (mid-Apr to late Oct)

Pets: Leashed pets permitted

Activities: Swimming, hiking, hunting

Management: US Army Corps of Engineers, Pittsburgh District

Contact: (814) 755-3512; www.lrp.usace.army.mil/missions/recreation/lakes/tionesta-lake/. For reservations call toll-free (877) 444-6777 or visit recreation.gov.

Finding the campground: From Tionesta go 0.5 mile south on Route 36 and follow signs into the campground.

GPS coordinates: N41 48.472'/W79 44.861'

Other: This is a great spot from which to launch day trips into Allegheny National Forest.

About the campground: The smallest of Tionesta Lake's three campgrounds accessible by vehicle, it's located along the banks of Tionesta Creek at the upstream end of Tionesta Lake. Alcoholic beverages are prohibited.

Why it's worth a visit: Trying to lose your neighbors for a while? This campground is the place for you, providing the rustic camper with a less-expensive camping experience close to fishing and hunting opportunities.

Trout anglers love Tionesta Creek in spring; smallmouth bass anglers love it in summer. And aside from some occasional paddlers, there's typically not much in the way of boat traffic this far upstream. A number of the smaller tributary streams that flow into Tionesta Creek in this area hold native brook trout.

This campground still has some basic amenities in season, so you can enjoy a more backwoods kind of outing without having to go totally primitive.

34 Loleta Recreation Area

Location: South of Marienville

Season: Year-round; best access from about Apr 1 to Oct 20 (no winter maintenance)

Sites: 38, some ADA accessible

Maximum RV length: 50 feet for the lower loop; sites on the upper loop primarily for tents and smaller trailers

Facilities: Vault toilets (flush toilets and warm showers seasonally in the beach bathhouse), water, electricity, picnic tables, fire rings, volleyball courts, amphitheater, beach bathhouse

Fee per night: $$$-$$$$

Pets: Leashed pets permitted

Activities: Swimming, hiking, fishing, hunting

Management: Allegheny National Forest

Contact: (814) 723-5150; www.fs.usda.gov/allegheny/. For reservations call (814) 444-6777 or visit www.recreation.gov. Some first-come, first-served sites are also available.

Finding the campground: From Marienville go south on Route 2005/Forest Street (between the Pennzoil Station and the Bucktail Hotel) for 6 miles until you see the sign for the campground.

GPS coordinates: N41 40.167'/W79 08.333'

Other: Two organized group tenting areas are available.

About the campground: Located on the east branch of Millstone Creek, the campground consists of two loops, one on each side of Loleta Road. The sites are spacious, well shaded, and screened from one another by vegetation.

Why it's worth a visit: Loleta Recreation Area is listed on the National Register of Historic Places. It occupies the spot where a logging town existed for about twenty-five years around the turn of the twentieth century. There were a large sawmill, a shingle factory, a broom handle factory, and a rail connection here then. When the hills were stripped bare of trees, as was the practice before anyone was talking about sustainability, the town was dismantled and deserted. A dozen years later the federal government bought the land and set Civilian Conservation Corps crews to work landscaping, rebuilding a pond, and constructing a bathhouse, swimming area, and picnic shelters. That work can still be seen in the dam's stonework and the log construction of the old bathhouse.

You can also explore a 3-mile hiking trail that begins and ends at the campground and passes a scenic overlook of Millstone Valley. Nearby you can explore some more recent man-made work at Buzzard Swamp—more visitor-friendly than its name would imply—which has a 9.6-mile network of trails running around a series of ponds built for waterfowl. It's perfect for hiking or mountain biking as well as fishing.

35 Cook Forest State Park

Location: Northeast of Clarion

Season: Mid-Apr to mid-Oct

Sites: 205, some ADA accessible

Maximum RV length: 50 feet

Facilities: Flush toilets, showers (seasonal), water, electricity, sanitary dump station (seasonal), picnic tables, fire rings, coin-operated laundry, environmental center

Fee per night: $$$-$$$$

Pets: Permitted at some sites

Activities: Hiking, biking, horseback riding, boating, environmental education programs, fishing, hunting

Roots, like so many arms with fingers, cling to a rocky outcrop in Cook Forest State Park.

Management: Pennsylvania Department of Conservation and Natural Resources

Contact: (814) 744-8407; www.dcnr.state.pa.us/stateparks/findapark/cookforest/index.htm. For reservations call toll-free (888) 727-2757 or visit VisitPaParks.com.

Finding the campground: Heading west on I-80, take exit 60 and follow Route 66 north to Leeper. Turn right (east) onto Route 36 and continue south for 7 miles to the park.

GPS coordinates: N41 33.699'/W79 22.336'

Other: This park has 20 rustic cabins for rent as well as an organized group tenting area. The Sawmill Craft Center and Theater offers displays, a gift shop, classes, and performances.

About the campground: Although the campground is open nine months out of the year, the shower houses are not. Numbers 1 and 2 are open from mid-April to mid-October; 3 and 4 are open from mid-May to mid-September. The dump station also closes in mid-October.

Why it's worth a visit: The area occupied by this very popular park was once known as the "Black Forest" because its towering trees completely shaded the forest floor from the sun. Amazingly that's still the case in places today. In a state that was once all but completely logged over, Cook Forest is home to some of the most impressive stands of old-growth timber anywhere. It boasts some of the tallest white pines and hemlocks on the East Coast, so a hike through the Forest Cathedral, a National Natural Landmark, is a must-do. Be sure to walk to the Seneca Point Overlook and climb the 90-foot fire tower nearby too.

While you're at it, check out some of the history here. The Log Cabin Inn, the park's environmental center, is a large log building crafted in 1934 by the Civilian Conservation Corps. It houses wildlife displays and old logging tools. The Indian and River Cabins are also on the National Register of Historic Places. There's some very nice canoeing to be done on the Clarion River and some good trout fishing to be had in Toms Run.

36 Clear Creek State Park

Location: North of Brookville
Season: Mid-Apr to mid-Dec
Sites: 52, some ADA accessible
Maximum RV length: 40 feet
Facilities: Flush toilets, showers, water, electricity, sanitary dump station, picnic tables, fire rings, nine-hole disc golf course, concrete basketball court
Fee per night: $$$–$$$$

Canoers, swimmers, and picnickers play on the Clarion River very near Clear Creek State Park.

Pets: Permitted at some sites

Activities: Swimming, hiking, environmental education programs, fishing, hunting

Management: Pennsylvania Department of Conservation and Natural Resources

Contact: (814) 752-2368; www.dcnr.state.pa.us/stateparks/findapark/clearcreek/index.htm. For reservations call toll-free (888) 727-2757 or visit VisitPaParks.com.

Finding the campground: From Brookville go west on US 322 until you can turn north onto Route 36. Go 8 miles and turn right (east) onto Route 949. Turn left onto Clear Creek Park Road and continue to the campground.

GPS coordinates: N41 33.192'/W79 10.098'

Other: This park has 22 rustic cabins and 2 yurts for rent and has campsites designed specifically for canoers and kayakers paddling the Clarion River. Maximum stay in these sites is 1 night.

About the campground: The main campground is divided into two loops separated by Clear Creek.

Why it's worth a visit: Located as close as it is to the more famous Cook Forest State Park, Clear Creek sometimes gets overlooked. That's too bad. You can swim at a small man-made lake, and there's some exceptional hiking to be had on trails leading to scenic overlooks and passing by and through rhododendron and mountain laurel that flowers in early June. But the park's main attraction is the Clarion River. It's a great river to float in a canoe, kayak, or even tube, especially in early summer, before water levels can get too low. You can bring your own boat or rent one from one of the many liveries nearby. Either way, be sure to bring a fishing rod with you; trout and small-mouth bass are plentiful and fun to catch.

If you want to see something unique, ask park staff about the rocks made famous by Douglas Stahlman. He spent the early years of the twentieth century inscribing Bible verses, dates, and personal beliefs on more than 530 rocks and trees in this area. People used to visit specific rocks for years thereafter to pray about subjects such as faith, guidance, love, and health. Stahlman eventually wound up in a Pittsburgh mental institution, but the local historical society still leads trips to his rocks all these years later.

37 Twin Lakes Recreation Area

Location: South of Kane

Season: Apr 15 to Dec 15; best access through Oct 20 (no winter maintenance)

Sites: 48, all ADA accessible

Maximum length: 28 feet

Facilities: Flush and rustic toilets, warm showers, water, electricity, sanitary dump station, picnic tables, fire rings, bathhouse, seasonal camp store

Fee per night: $$-$$$$

Pets: Leashed pets permitted

Activities: Swimming, hiking, fishing, hunting

Management: Allegheny National Forest

Contact: (814) 723-5150; www.fs.usda.gov/allegheny/. For reservations call (814) 444-6777 or visit www.recreation.gov. Some first-come, first-served sites are also available.

Finding the campground: Take Route 321 south from Kane for about 6 miles. Turn right onto FR 191 and follow it for about 2 miles to the campground.

GPS coordinates: N41 61.222'/W78 76.083'

Other: So where's the "twin" at Twin Lakes? It was never built. The existing lake was built by the Civilian Conservation Corps in 1936, but the money for its twin was diverted to create Loleta Recreation Area instead.

About the campground: The entrance road leading to this campground requires driving beneath a railroad underpass with just 10 feet of clearance, so your RV has to be shorter than that to get in. There's also an organized group tent site.

Why it's worth a visit: This is another of those campgrounds that sprang up after industry laid waste to this piece of countryside. McKean Chemical Co. made wood alcohol here in the early twentieth century, and the site had factories, stores, row houses, and a splash dam, used to bolster the water supply. When that business passed from the scene in the 1920s, the federal government bought the land and created the beautiful recreation area that exists today.

Twin Lakes offers a little bit of everything and draws very big, consistent crowds as a result. It has a small spring-fed, trout-stocked lake that's popular with families and is especially productive in spring. Mill Creek offers angling for native trout. You can also swim, play, and hike on the Twin Lakes and Black Cherry Trails. The latter is an interpretive walk offering forty educational displays along the way.

38 Tracy Ridge Recreation Area

Location: West of Bradford
Season: Apr 15 to Dec 15
Sites: 119, some ADA accessible
Maximum RV length: 50 feet
Facilities: Vault toilets, water, sanitary dump station, picnic tables, fire rings
Fee per night: $-$$
Pets: Leashed pets permitted
Activities: Hiking, cross-country skiing, hunting
Management: Allegheny National Forest
Contact: (814) 723-5150; www.fs.usda.gov/allegheny/. For reservations call (814) 444-6777 or visit www.recreation.gov. Some first-come, first-served sites are also available.
Finding the campground: From Bradford head west on Route 346 for about 16 miles. Turn left (south) onto Route 321 and go about 2 miles; the campground will be on your right.
GPS coordinates: N41 94.417'/W78 87.611'
Other: Groups can reserve any one of three loops at this campground.
About the campground: This campground sits atop a hill in a mature oak stand, so all the sites are shaded. They're well spaced too, so you'll have some elbow room.
Why it's worth a visit: Whereas many of the campgrounds in Allegheny National Forest are by design close to the water, this is an exception. Tracy Ridge is meant for hikers. The trailhead is here for a nearly 34-mile system of trails through Tracy Ridge Recreation Area, one of the few roadless areas in the forest.

A terrific day hike takes you from the flat ridgetop campground at 2,245 feet above sea level to a valley at 1,328 feet—the normal pool level of Allegheny Reservoir—and back, with lots of cool rock formations along the way. It's especially beautiful in fall, when the leaves have changed colors.

Be aware that there are some steep climbs though; you'll want to be in shape if you tackle a long loop. The Tracy Ridge trail system is marked with gray diamonds; portions of the North Country National Scenic Trail, which pass through, are marked in blue. You can also backpack and camp here.

39 Elk State Park

Location: Northeast of Johnsonburg
Season: Mid-Apr to early Oct
Sites: 41, 9 walk-in only
Maximum RV length: 70 feet
Facilities: Flush toilets, warm showers, water, sanitary dump station, picnic tables, fire rings
Fee per night: $$$–$$$$
Pets: Leashed pets permitted
Activities: Boating, waterskiing, tubing, hiking, biking, fishing, hunting
Management: US Army Corps of Engineers, Pittsburgh District
Contact: For information on the lake itself, call (814) 965-2065; or visit www.lrp.usace.army.mil/Missions/Recreation/Lakes/East-Branch-Clarion-River-Lake/. For information on the park, call (814) 778-5467 or visit www.dcnr.pa.gov/StateParks/FindAPark/ElkStatePark/Pages/default.aspx. No reservations accepted; it's first come, first served.
Finding the campground: From Johnsonburg go north on US 219 for 6.6 miles. At the blinking light in Wilcox, turn right onto Clarion Street, which in 0.8 mile becomes Rassalas Road. Travel 1.8 miles and turn right onto Glen Hazel Road. Go 4 miles and turn left onto Kilgus Road. Continue 1 mile to the dam.
GPS coordinates: N41 56.049' / W78 59.893'
Other: Alcoholic beverages are prohibited.
About the campground: Formerly known as East Branch Clarion River Lake, this state park surrounds a US Army Corps of Engineers water. A newer finished restroom and shower facility awaits campers here. Most sites are situated under mature shade trees.
Why it's worth a visit: Featuring a 1,371-acre lake in the upper reaches of the scenic Clarion River valley, this facility is unique in terms of one of the species it is home to. The lake's cold, deep water is one of the few places in Pennsylvania outside Lake Erie to hold lake trout. They get big too: upward of 33 inches. You'll find muskies, tiger muskies, smallmouth bass, and rock bass as well.

If you really want to have some fun on this lake, which is open to unlimited horsepower, zip around with your skis or tubes, then tuck yourself away into one of its many bays and coves for a picnic on the water. Another benefit to staying at this campground is its location near the towns of St. Marys and Emporium. That makes it a great launching pad for viewing the state's elk herd, which numbers more than 800 animals and is concentrated locally.

40 Parker Dam State Park

Location: East of DuBois
Season: Second Fri in Apr through mid-Dec

Tourists watch a cow elk wearing a radio collar at Winslow Hill viewing area, easily accessible from nearby Parker Dam State Park.

Sites: 109, some ADA accessible
Maximum RV length: 40 feet
Facilities: Flush toilets, warm showers, water, electricity, sewage (some full-service sites), sanitary dump station, picnic tables, fire rings, coin-operated laundry, seasonal camp store
Fee per night: $$$–$$$$
Pets: A maximum of 2 domestic pets permitted at some sites
Activities: Boating, swimming, geocaching, hiking, biking, environmental education programs, fishing, hunting, special weekends for volunteers
Management: Pennsylvania Department of Conservation and Natural Resources
Contact: (814) 765-0630; www.dcnr.state.pa.us/stateparks/findapark/parkerdam/index.htm. For reservations call toll-free (888) 727-2757 or visit VisitPaParks.com.
Finding the campground: From DuBois follow Route 255 north for 12.2 miles. Turn right onto Route 153 east and go 2.5 miles. Turn left onto Mud Run Road and go 3.3 miles to the park.
GPS coordinates: N41 19.706' / W78 50.650'
Other: This park has 17 cabins for rent as well as an organized group tenting area. It also plays host to Woodhick Weekend on the Sunday of Labor Day weekend, when park visitors can roll logs, use a crosscut saw, and compete in other events that hearken back to the area's logging past. There's even a Woodhick and Woodchick of the Year competition.

About the campground: Parts of the campground have been designated as pet-friendly. Sites range from walk-in tent-only sites to wooded nonelectric ones to more open full-service sites. All sites are back-in.

Why it's worth a visit: This is a great park for doing some exploring. It's got 16 miles of trails, many of them winding into and through the adjacent Moshannon State Forest, so you can see black bears, deer, rattlesnakes, bobcats, coyotes, and all kinds of other wildlife. It's also the western trailhead for the 73-mile Quehanna Trail System. There's some pleasant fishing and boating here as well.

What's really special though is that Parker Dam State Park is only a 50-minute drive from the heart of Pennsylvania's elk range; no other park or campground is closer. If you want to see elk, you'll drive from the campground to the most famous elk-watching point, Winslow Hill, located on State Game Land 311 between Benezette and Grant. There you can see elk weighing up to 1,000 pounds wandering among houses, past the local post office, and along roads. September and October are prime viewing time, when the mating season, or "rut," has the bulls bugling in high-pitched tones to call females.

The nearby Elk Country Visitor Center has interactive exhibits and movies, wildlife viewing stations, hiking trails, and more, all centered on a conservation theme.

41 Simon B. Elliott State Park

Location: Northwest of Clearfield
Season: Early May to late Oct
Sites: 25, some ADA accessible
Maximum RV length: 40 feet
Facilities and activities: Flush toilets, water, sanitary dump station
Fee per night: $$-$$$$
Pets: A maximum of 2 domestic pets allowed per site
Activities: Hiking, fishing, hunting
Management: Pennsylvania Department of Conservation and Natural Resources
Contact: (814) 765-0630; www.dcnr.state.pa.us/stateparks/findapark/simonbelliott/index.htm. For reservations call toll-free (888) 727-2757 or visit www.VisitPaParks.com.
Finding the campground: It's located one mile north of I-80. Take the Clearfield exit, exit 111, and follow Route 153.
GPS coordinates: N41 11.273'/W78 52.611'
Other: This park, which also has 6 rustic cabins for rent, has been home to the annual High Country Arts and Crafts Fair for a quarter century. Put on by the local Elks Club, it features food, trolley rides, entertainment, and craft vendors.
About the campground: All sites are pet-friendly. This is rustic camping, with no electric hookups and no showers. All sites are back-in.
Why it's worth a visit: This is another of those parks that's a relatively tiny patch of woods surrounded by a much, much larger state forest. There's hiking on Old Horse Trail, which winds past a small pond. Boundaries between park and forest mean nothing here, so if you stay at this campground, you have a huge wooded playground at your disposal.

If you're into fishing, you could spend a lot of time walking small streams and casting for native trout without ever having to hit the same water twice. And if you want to hike, you can follow the North Fork and Rattlesnake Trails out of the park and into Moshannon State Forest, from where you can spin off in many directions.

42 Curwensville Lake

Location: Southwest of Clearfield
Season: May 1 to the end of Oct
Sites: 51, some ADA accessible and some primitive tent sites
Maximum RV length: 60 feet
Facilities: Flush toilets, warm showers, water, electricity, playgrounds, boat launch, ball fields
Fee per night: $$$-$$$$
Pets: Leashed pets permitted
Activities: Boating, waterskiing, tubing, swimming, hiking, mountain biking, fishing, hunting
Management: Clearfield County
Contact: (814) 236-2320; http://curwensvillelake.com. For reservations call toll-free (800) 326-9051. Some overflow sites are available on a first-come, first-served basis.
Finding the campground: From Clearfield head south on Route 153/Second Street for 1.3 miles. Second Street becomes Route 879 West/Clearfield Curwensville Highway; continue 4.6 miles. Turn left onto Filbert Street; go 0.1 mile and continue following Route 453/Susquehanna Avenue for 3 miles. Turn right onto Lake Drive and go 0.8 mile to the park.
GPS coordinates: N40 94.350'/W78 53.911'
Other: Unlike a lot of campgrounds, this one hosts a number of special events throughout the year that are not tied strictly to nature. There's a Memorial Day weekend craft show, a Wheels at the Lake car show, and a "campground yard sale."
About the campground: This is a US Army Corps of Engineers lake, but the campground is run by Clearfield County.
Why it's worth a visit: Curwensville Lake is a 790-acre impoundment located on the West Branch Susquehanna River. There are no horsepower restrictions on this lake, so that makes it a watery racetrack of sorts—a favorite for people looking to water-ski, tube, or ride personal watercraft.

Anglers ply the waters too. The lake offers pretty decent fishing for largemouth and small-mouth bass, muskies, perch, and bluegills. Canoers and kayaks even do their thing in some of the smaller coves.

Away from the water there are a number of trails used by hikers and mountain bikers.

43 Black Moshannon State Park

Location: East of Philipsburg
Season: Mid-Apr to mid-Dec
Sites: 73, some ADA accessible
Maximum RV length: 40 feet

A water lily, not yet completely open, floats on the surface of Black Moshannon Lake in Black Moshannon State Park.

Facilities: Flush toilets, showers, water, electricity, sanitary dump station, picnic tables, fire rings, swimming beach; hiking trails, mountain biking trails, coin-operated laundry, camp store, kayak and boat rentals

Fee per night: $$$-$$$$

Pets: Permitted at some sites

Activities: Boating (unpowered and electric motors only), swimming, hiking, mountain biking, environmental education programs, fishing, hunting, birding

Management: Pennsylvania Department of Conservation and Natural Resources

Contact: (814) 342-5960; www.dcnr.state.pa.us/stateparks/findapark/blackmoshanon/index .htm. For reservations call toll-free (888) 727-2757 or visit VisitPaParks.com.

Finding the campground: From Philipsburg follow US 322 east. Turn left onto Route 504 east and travel 8 miles to the park.

GPS coordinates: N40 91.518'/W78 06.072'

Other: This park has 13 rustic cabins, 6 modern cabins, and 2 deluxe camping cottages for rent and offers an organized group tenting area.

About the campground: The campground is a loop with a couple of spurs. The nonelectric sites at the end of one spur offer the most privacy; sites near the camp store are a short walk from the swimming beach.

Why it's worth a visit: Water is supposed to be blue, right? Not here. Black Moshannon Lake is fed by clear springs, but that water passes through several bogs populated with sphagnum moss and other plants on the way to the lake. As a result the water ends up a dark brown by the time it gets to the lake. Imagine water poured through a tea bag and you can understand the effect.

Paddling the dark waters in a canoe or kayak, especially when you get to the sections covered in floating wildflowers, is a uniquely gorgeous experience. An elevated walking path that extends into the bog allows you to experience it on foot. This is also a wonderful place to hike if you like a big-woods feel—the park has 20 miles of trails of its own and is surrounded by 43,000 acres of state forest. The 1.2-mile Sleepy Hollow Trail is a favorite in spring, when wildflowers are in bloom. The 2.1-mile Star Hollow Trail offers easier walking and some beautiful views of the lake. Moss-Hanne Trail is the park's longest at 7.7 miles. It's difficult and wet in sections, though volunteers who are members of the Friends of Black Moshannon group are continuously building wooden footpaths in the wettest areas and otherwise making improvements. Either way, if you like to pick wild blueberries—as do the park's bears—it's well worthwhile.

44 Bald Eagle State Park

Location: Southwest of Lock Haven

Season: Mid-Apr to mid-Dec

Sites: 160; some sites ADA accessible. There are 34 walk-in sites and 34 reserved for camping vehicles in a primitive area.

Maximum RV length: 40 feet

Facilities: Flush and/or vault toilets (depending on site), showers, water, electricity, sanitary dump station, picnic tables, fire rings, swimming beach, marina, hiking trails, picnic areas, playgrounds

Fee per night: $$$-$$$$

Pets: Permitted at some sites

A bullfrog peers out of Frog Pond at Bald Eagle State Park.

Activities: Boating, swimming, hiking, environmental education programs, fishing, hunting
Management: Pennsylvania Department of Conservation and Natural Resources
Contact: (814) 625-2775; www.dcnr.state.pa.us/stateparks/findapark/baldeagle/index.htm. For reservations call toll-free (888) 727-2757 or visit VisitPaParks.com.
Finding the campground: From I-80 west take exit 158 to Route 150 and follow it north for about 10 miles. Look for signs for the park.

From I-80 east take exit 178 to US 220 north; turn right onto Route 150 south and continue about 13 miles. Look for signs for the park.
GPS coordinates: N41 03.550' / W77 64.708' for Russell T. Letterman; N41 02.900' / W77 62.776' for Primitive.
Other: This park also has 3 cottages, 1 deluxe cottage, and 2 yurts for rent and has the state park system's only nature inn.
About the campground: The Russell T. Letterman Campground features more modern amenities such as showers and flush toilets, but is also more exposed to the sun. Some of the sites on the outside edges of the campground's two loops offer the most space. The Primitive Camping Area can handle tents and smaller RVs and is more wooded, but it has just vault toilets.
Why it's worth a visit: This is a big park—about 5,900 acres—that has 1,730-acre Foster Joseph Sayers Lake as its centerpiece. The lake is nestled between steep ridges and a very popular fishery, especially for those who pursue black crappies, bluegills, and largemouth bass.

There's a lot more to do here than just fish though. There's a nice network of nearly 15 miles of trails and a beach with playground and snack bar. Wildlife watching is popular too. White-tailed deer are common in the park's wood and field edges, and frogs and salamanders abound at Frog Pond. There's even a hiking trail that winds through an area designed specifically to attract butterflies.

Birders come here because it's a citizen research station of sorts. There's what's called an "eBird Trail Tracker" kiosk at the Nature Inn. Operated in cooperation with Cornell University's Laboratory of Ornithology, it details what birds are being seen at the park and where; offers photo, audio, and video life histories of those species; and allows birders to record their own observations. Any information you submit about what you saw is accessible to scientists and others tracking birds across the country.

45 Ravensburg State Park

Location: South of Jersey Shore
Season: First Fri in May through the last Sat in Sept
Sites: 21, for tents only
Maximum length: N/A
Facilities: Vault toilets, warm showers, water, picnic tables, fire ring
Fee per night: $$–$$$$
Pets: Permitted at some sites
Activities: Hiking, fishing
Management: Pennsylvania Department of Conservation and Natural Resources
Contact: (570) 966-1455; www.dcnr.state.pa.us/stateparks/findapark/ravensburg/index.htm. No reservations accepted; it's first come, first served.
Finding the campground: Follow Route 44 south from Jersey Shore for 3.7 miles. Turn right (south) onto Route 880 and go 3.7 miles to the park.
GPS coordinates: N41 11.399'/W77 24.131'
Other: This park was named for the ravens that once roosted on the famous rock ledges at the park's southern end. They're still fairly common today and distinguishable from crows by their larger size and deeper, groan-like call.
About the campground: This campground is for tents only. Sites 16 to 21 are the most private.
Why it's worth a visit: This tiny 78-acre park is located in a steep gorge. That makes it one of the few places in this part of the state that likely wasn't ever logged over. Don't expect to see towering timber though. The steep, rocky mountainsides aren't especially hospitable, so stubborn, stunted oaks predominate. Interspersed among those trees are rock formations, including Castle Rocks—spires of sandstone said to look like the towers of an ancient castle. The rocks are all that's left of a sandstone rock face; frost has split the rock and at times forced parts of it to fall away, leaving the "castle" pieces. You can get to Castle Rocks via Mid State Trail in the southern end of the park. Before heading out, be sure to pick up a copy of the geology guide available at the park office. It explains more about the rocks' origins.

The park is especially pretty in June, when the mountain laurel is in bloom, and again in fall, when the foliage is at its peak. Rauchtown Run and its tributaries provide good wild trout fishing in spring and fall.

46 Little Pine State Park

Location: North of Jersey Shore
Season: 8 months; the first weekend in Apr to mid-Dec
Sites: 99, 6 walk-in only and some ADA accessible
Maximum RV length: 50 feet
Facilities: Flush toilets, warm showers, water, electricity, picnic table, fire ring, sanitary dump station, boat launch, rail-trail for hiking and biking
Fee per night: $$$-$$$$
Pets: Permitted at some sites
Activities: Boating, swimming, hiking, biking, fishing, hunting, environmental education programs, annual autumn festival
Management: Pennsylvania Department of Conservation and Natural Resources
Contact: (570) 753-6000; www.dcnr.state.pa.us/stateparks/findapark/littlepine/index.htm. For reservations call toll-free (888) 727-2757 or visit VisitPaParks.com.
Finding the campground: From Jersey Shore follow US 220 south for about 3 miles. Turn right (north) onto Route 44 toward Waterville and go about 11 miles. Turn right onto Little Pine Creek Road and go 4 miles to the campground.
GPS coordinates: N41 35.195'/W77 35.512'
Other: The park also offers cottages and yurts for rent and has an organized group tenting area.
About the campground: This campground, which has a cemetery at its center, does not offer a lot of privacy between sites. But those that face Little Pine Creek are among the nicest.
Why it's worth a visit: Most of the facilities in this park were wiped out in 1972 when Hurricane Agnes roared through, sending water over the lake's dam for the first time. Today Little Pine State Park offers some good opportunities for the angler, with wild and stocked trout available in Little Pine Creek and smallmouth bass and other warmwater species available in the park's 94-acre lake. There's also an observation deck for viewing the bald eagles that have nested here for a decade.

A real highlight of the park is its hiking opportunities. Level trails with lots of wildflowers and wildlife are perfect for families with children. Rugged walks like the Panther Hollow Trail lead to scenic vistas, rock outcroppings, and solitude. If you've got kids, be sure to follow Lake Shore Trail and spend time exploring the lake's upper end. Its extensive shallows make it home to all kinds of frogs, turtles, and birds, including great blue herons, as well as mink, muskrats, and otters.

47 Hyner Run State Park

Location: East of Renovo
Season: Mid-Apr to mid-Dec
Sites: 30, some ADA accessible
Maximum RV length: 56 feet
Facilities: Flush toilets, showers, water, electricity, sanitary dump station, picnic tables, fire rings, children's play area
Fee per night: $$$-$$$$

Pets: Permitted at some sites

Activities: Swimming, hiking, fishing, hunting, environmental education programs

Management: Pennsylvania Department of Conservation and Natural Resources

Contact: (570) 923-6000; www.dcnr.state.pa.us/stateparks/findapark/hynerrun/index.htm. For reservations call toll-free (888) 727-2757 or visit VisitPaParks.com.

Finding the campground: From Renovo go east on Route 120 for about 6 miles. Turn left onto Hyner Run Road, which becomes Hyner Mountain Road, and travel 2 miles to the park. The campground is in the park on Hyner Park Road.

GPS coordinates: N41 35.753' / W77 62.817'

Other: This park, which also has one modern cabin for rent, is a great base from which to visit nearby Hyner View State Park. The scenic overlook there, considered one of the most beautiful in the state for its gorgeous view of the West Branch Susquehanna River, is a favorite launching point for hang gliders.

About the campground: This is a loop campground, with a shower house and playground closest to the nonelectric sites.

Why it's worth a visit: Originally designed to serve as a camp for Civilian Conservation Corps workers, this area later became a pine tree plantation before ultimately becoming a park. It's a tiny bit of civilization within a wilderness. Entirely surrounded by Sproul State Forest, the state's largest, it has a large swimming pool and a children's play area and is host to environmental education programs twice a month in summer.

If you like your attractions more natural, the park offers some excellent fishing for trout, both stocked and wild. And while there are no hiking trails within the tiny park itself, it is the western trailhead for the 90-mile Donut Hole Trail.

48 Kettle Creek State Park

Location: Northwest of Renovo

Season: Early Apr to mid-Dec for the larger, Lower Campground along Kettle Creek; mid-Apr to mid-Oct for the smaller Upper Campground

Sites: 41 in Lower Campground, 27 in Upper Campground

Maximum RV length: 45 feet

Facilities: Flush toilets, warm showers, water, electricity, sanitary dump station, picnic tables, fire rings, boat launch

Fee per night: $$$-$$$$

Pets: Permitted at some sites in the Upper Campground

Activities: Boating, hiking, mountain biking, horseback riding, fishing, environmental education programs

Management: Pennsylvania Department of Conservation and Natural Resources

Contact: (570) 923-6004; www.dcnr.state.pa.us/stateparks/findapark/kettlecreek/index.htm. For reservations call toll-free (888) 727-2757 or visit VisitPaParks.com.

Finding the campground: From Renovo go southwest on Route 120 for about 6.5 miles. At Westport turn right onto Kettle Creek Road and go a little less than 0.5 mile. Both campgrounds are on the left side of the road.

GPS coordinates: N41 36.744'/W77 93.444' for Upper Campground; N41 34.163'/W77 91.083' for Lower Campground

Other: There are 22 miles of horseback riding trails in the forest surrounding this park.

About the campground: The nonelectric sites at the upper section are the least crowded. The electric sites at both the upper and lower campgrounds are lined side by side, though many of those at the lower section do have the benefit of facing Kettle Creek.

Why it's worth a visit: This remote, nearly 1,800-acre park lies in a valley surrounded by mountainous wilderness. It's gorgeous, as the drive in showcases immediately. The view of Kettle Creek, flowing at the base of steep-sided mountains, will take your breath away, especially when spring first turns things green and fall changes the leaves to orange, red, and yellow.

The park is also a great place to see wildlife, some of it the kind that you won't find in too many places in Pennsylvania. This part of the state is home to as many black bears as anywhere in the state, along with white-tailed deer, turkeys, otters, fishers, and elk. The 167-acre Kettle Creek Reservoir attracts migrating waterfowl, including loons, grebes, and gulls, in spring and fall. Bald eagles, flashy wood ducks, great blue herons, kingfishers, and mergansers are year-round residents. Woodpeckers patrol the woods year-round, and the park's field edges are home to bluebirds, goldfinches, indigo buntings, and other species. Quietly canoeing or kayaking on the lake often allows you to get closer to some of that wildlife than others might—one shoreline is so steep that it limits foot access—while also catching trout, bass, and panfish.

49 Sinnemahoning State Park

Location: Southeast of Emporium

Season: Second weekend in Apr to late Dec

Sites: 35, some ADA accessible and some walk-in only

Maximum length: 75 feet

Facilities: Flush toilets, warm showers, water, electricity, sanitary dump station, picnic tables, fire rings, boat launch, wildlife center

Fee per night: $$$-$$$$

Pets: Permitted in some sites

Activities: Boating (unpowered and electric motors only), hiking, fishing, hunting, environmental education programs, including pontoon boat rides

Management: Pennsylvania Department of Conservation and Natural Resources

Contact: (814) 647-8401; www.dcnr.state.pa.us/stateparks/findapark/sinnemahoning/index .htm. For reservations call toll-free (888) 727-2757 or visit VisitPaParks.com.

Finding the campground: The park is located of Route 872, 8 miles north of its junction with Route 120 in Sinnemahoning.

GPS coordinates: N41 46.510'/W78 06.370'

Other: The park also has a two-story cabin for rent.

About the campground: This campground can handle larger RVs than most Pennsylvania parks and features a nice amount of space in between sites.

Why it's worth a visit: Opportunities to see wildlife are a big reason to visit Sinnemahoning State Park. There are bald eagles, otters, a growing elk herd (look for them in spring along the Low Land

Trail, at the Forty Maples picnic area, and at the park's wildlife viewing area), deer, bears, coyotes, bobcats, songbirds, butterflies, and more. To enhance all that, and because this park is at the very center of the Pennsylvania Wilds, it's home to a 9,300-square-foot wildlife center featuring interactive exhibits, displays, and programs. Designers are hoping it will help spread the park system's conservation message.

While you're here, be sure to fish for trout and smallmouth bass in the First Fork Sinnemahoning Creek. There's a delayed-harvest, artificial-lures-only section of stream at the park's northern end. If you've got family that will want to play while you cast, try the Forty Maples area. It's a wonderfully scenic picnic spot with some trails to hike too.

50 Ole Bull State Park

Location: South of Galeton
Season: Year-round
Sites: 77, some ADA accessible
Maximum RV length: 40 feet
Facilities: Flush toilets, warm showers, water, electricity, sanitary dump station, picnic tables, fire rings
Fee per night: $$–$$$
Pets: Permitted in Campground 2
Activities: Swimming, hiking, cross-country skiing, snowmobiling, fishing, hunting, environmental education programs
Management: Pennsylvania Department of Conservation and Natural Resources
Contact: (814) 435-5000; www.dcnr.state.pa.us/stateparks/findapark/olebull/index.htm. For reservations call toll-free (888) 727-2757 or visit VisitPaParks.com.
Finding the campground: From Galeton follow Route 144 south for 17 miles to the park and campground.
GPS coordinates: N41 54.037'/W77 71.377'
Other: A 1.5-story log cabin is also available for rent. There are also 2 rustic organized group tenting sites.
About the campground: This is one of a handful of state park campgrounds that are open year-round. It consists of two loops, with those located along Kettle Creek in both Areas 1 and 2 among the prettiest.
Why it's worth a visit: This park is named for a Norwegian violinist, Ole Bornemann Bull, who tried to establish a colony here in the 1850s. The colony dissolved after one year of extreme hardship— you can read an account of his efforts at the park office. The Castle Vista Trail will take you past the remains of the foundation of the home Bull started to build but never finished. The Daugherty Loop Trail follows old railroad and logging grades through the kind of mature forest that once led some people to also call this area the "Black Forest" because of its canopy of huge, sunlight-blocking trees. This tiny park—only 132 acres—also offers good fishing for brook, brown, and rainbow trout, with a special section of stream set aside specifically for children and people with disabilities. There's even a beach that dates to the 1930s.

51 Leonard Harrison State Park

Location: West of Wellsboro
Season: Second Sat in Apr to late Oct
Sites: 25
Maximum RV length: 100 feet
Facilities: Flush toilets, warm showers, water, electricity, sanitary dump station, picnic tables, fire rings, gift shop, nature center
Fee per night: $$$-$$$$
Pets: No pets allowed
Activities: Hiking, fishing, hunting, environmental education programs
Management: Pennsylvania Department of Conservation and Natural Resources
Contact: (570) 923-6004; www.dcnr.state.pa.us/stateparks/findapark/leonardharrison/index .htm. For reservations call toll-free (888) 727-2757 or visit VisitPaParks.com.
Finding the campground: From Wellsboro head west on Route 660 for about 10 miles to the park. Look for the campground entrance, marked with a sign, on your left before you get to the park's main day-use area.
GPS coordinates: N41 69.861'/W77 44.902'

The view of Pennsylvania's Grand Canyon from Leonard Harrison State Park is spectacular.

Other: Located on the eastern rim of "Pennsylvania's Grand Canyon," this park has a bronze monument to the men of the Civilian Conservation Corps, who helped build it.

About the campground: This small campground offers a good bit of privacy; the electric sites have the most space. A couple of the nonelectric sites, numbers 18 and 19, are also off by themselves.

Why it's worth a visit: This park offers the absolute best views of Pennsylvania's Grand Canyon and correspondingly draws bigger crowds than Colton Point State Park, which is on the opposite rim. It helps that the overlooks are just a short walk from the parking lot. You enter through a gateway of sorts, which separates the park's small visitor center from its souvenir store, and immediately the canyon is there in front of you in all its breathtaking glory. It figures to be there as is for a long while too. The canyon is managed as a state park natural area these days, meaning that it will be kept in its natural state for future generations. You can learn more about that at the nature center, which is open summer through fall for self-guided visits. From April through October an environmental educator in residence provides a variety of programs, focusing on everything from old-fashioned cider making to campfire tales to astronomy.

If you want to get away from the crowds, there are trails that lead to scenic vistas and spectacular views, such as the rugged but particularly beautiful Turkey Path Trail.

52 Colton Point State Park

Location: 5 miles south of US 6 at Ansonia, on Colton Point Road
Season: Early May to mid-Oct
Sites: 21, 6 walk-in only
Maximum length: 30 feet
Facilities: Vault toilets, picnic tables, fire rings
Fee per night: $$-$$$$
Pets: No pets allowed
Activities: Boating, hiking, fishing, hunting, environmental education programs
Management: Pennsylvania Department of Conservation and Natural Resources
Contact: (570) 724-3061; www.dcnr.state.pa.us/stateparks/findapark/coltonpoint/index.htm. No reservations accepted; it's first come, first served.
Finding the campground: From Ansonia, head west on US 6 for less than a mile. Turn left onto Colton Road and follow it to the park and the campground.
GPS coordinates: N41 70.795' / W77 46.760'
Other: This park is almost directly across the Pine Creek Gorge from another state park, Leonard Harrison. It has an organized group tenting area.
About the campground: All the campground's sites offer decent privacy. Its ten walk-in sites—particularly numbers 15, 16, 17, and 18—offer the most solitude.
Why it's worth a visit: Stand at Colton Point on the rim of the Pine Creek Gorge and you'll have no doubt why they call this "Pennsylvania's Grand Canyon." The view is spectacular—ridges of solid green in summer and oranges, golds, and reds in fall—reaching from the sky to the blue ribbon of Pine Creek 800 feet below.

There are many ways to enjoy the canyon. Trails lead from the canyon rim to the stream, and seasonally, before water levels drop, you can paddle the stream, which features a couple of Class II or III rapids. Perhaps the best way to experience the canyon from the bottom up, though, is to

Pine Creek flows below an overlook at Colton Point State Park.

bike the 62-mile Pine Creek Trail. Declared by some to be one of the ten best rail-trails in the entire country, it's a limestone gravel pathway that leads past rock outcrops and waterfalls. You see a lot of wildlife from this trail, on it or crossing it too: black bears, bald eagles, timber rattlesnakes, white-tailed deer, otters, and ospreys, to name a few. There's some old-growth forest along the trail as well.

53 Lyman Run State Park

Location: East of Coudersport
Season: Second weekend in Apr to second weekend in Dec
Sites: 35, some ADA accessible and 6 walk-in only, at two campgrounds: Daggett Run and Lower Campground
Maximum RV length: 134 feet
Facilities: Flush toilets, warm showers, water, electricity, sanitary dump station (at Lower Campground only), picnic tables, fire rings, lantern hangers, boat launch, ATV trail
Fee per night: $$$-$$$$
Pets: Permitted at some sites
Activities: Boating, swimming, geocaching, hiking, fishing, hunting, environmental education programs
Management: Pennsylvania Department of Conservation and Natural Resources
Contact: (814) 435-1510; www.dcnr.state.pa.us/stateparks/findapark/lymanrun/index.htm. For reservations call toll-free (888) 727-2757 or visit VisitPaParks.com.
Finding the campground: From Coudersport go east on US 6 for about 4 miles. Turn right onto Route 44 east and go 11 miles. Take a slight left onto West Branch Road. Go 6 miles and turn left onto Lyman Run Road. Go about 2.5 miles to the park.
GPS coordinates: N41 72.844' / W77 76.209' for Daggett; N41 71.563' / W77 74.492' for Lower Campground
Other: This park was once home to a camp that housed German prisoners of war near the end of World War II.
About the campground: Both of the campgrounds at this park are relatively small, but there's lots of space between individual sites, more than is typical at some other parks. The walk-in sites are not too far off the road either.
Why it's worth a visit: There's some fine trout fishing to be had, especially early in spring, as well as 6 miles of hiking in Lyman Run. Wildcat Trail is a relatively short walk that goes past some massive old hemlock trees. Some of the 85-mile Susquehannock Trail, a loop that passes through some of the most rugged country in the Keystone State, also runs through here.

What sets this park apart from many others is that it's a stepping-off point for all-terrain vehicle use. There are 43 miles of ATV trails in Susquehannock State Forest, and Lyman Run has a parking area within walking distance of restrooms and a concession stand catering to riders. These are considered "summer" ATV trails, meaning they are open the Friday before Memorial Day to the last full weekend in September. Details on the trail, and all ATV trails on state forest land, can be found at www.dcnr.pa.gov/Recreation/WhatToDo/ATVRiding/pages/default.aspx.

54 Cherry Springs State Park

Location: West of Wellsboro
Season: Mid-Apr to Nov
Sites: 30
Maximum RV length: 81 feet
Facilities: Vault toilets, water, sanitary dump station, picnic tables, fire rings, lantern hangers
Fee per night: $$–$$$$
Pets: No pets allowed
Activities: Stargazing, hiking, mountain biking, hunting, environmental education programs
Management: Pennsylvania Department of Conservation and Natural Resources
Contact: (814) 435-5010; www.dcnr.state.pa.us/stateparks/findapark/cherrysprings/index.htm. No reservations accepted; it's first come, first served.
Finding the campground: From Wellsboro go west on Route 660, then continue onto Route 362 north. Turn left (west) onto US 6 at Ansonia. Go about 12.5 miles; turn onto West Street, which becomes West Branch Road. Go about 11 miles and turn right onto Route 44 north. The entrance to the campground is off Route 44.
GPS coordinates: N41 66.243'/W77 80.912'
Other: This park has hosted the Woodsmen's Carnival, a lumberjack competition, on the first weekend of each August since 1952. That weekend is by far the busiest of the year for the campground.
About the campground: Payment is made on the honor system. Envelopes can be picked up at the contact station just off Route 44.
Why it's worth a visit: Cherry Springs is famous all out of proportion to its size—only 48 acres—because it's surrounded by 262,000-acre Susquehannock State Forest and little else. That's the draw. The lack of any development over the past 200 years and the absence of resultant light pollution make Cherry Springs perhaps the best place on the entire Eastern Seaboard to get a look at the night skies. Astronomy buffs flock here to get views of stars, planets, and galaxies that just aren't available in many places. In fact the park has been designated a Gold Level International Dark Sky Park by the folks who measure such things. The park offers a large number of evening programs to teach visitors about the night skies, with those surrounding the Perseids meteor shower each August particularly popular.

If you have your own telescope and equipment and are a serious astronomer, the park rents four small observatories on a nightly basis. Just be aware that if you come here, the folks around you take their darkness seriously. There are all kinds of rules in place regarding the use of white light. Be courteous of others and obey the rules.

55 Patterson State Park

Location: South of Sweden Valley
Season: Mid-Apr to mid-Dec
Sites: 10, mostly for tents; some fit RVs
Maximum RV length: 40 feet
Facilities: Vault toilets, water, picnic tables, fire rings, picnic pavilions

Fee per night: $$-$$$$
Pets: No pets allowed
Activities: Hiking, mountain biking, hunting
Management: Pennsylvania Department of Conservation and Natural Resources
Contact: (814) 435-5010; www.dcnr.state.pa.us/stateparks/findapark/patterson/index.htm. No reservations accepted; it's first come, first served.
Finding the campground: From US 6 in Sweden Valley, turn south onto Route 44 and travel 6.5 miles. Route 44 goes right through the park.
GPS coordinates: N41 70.365' / W77 91.092'
Other: This park has two beautiful pavilions that are perfect for picnicking.
About the campground: The park is completely surrounded by Susquehannock State Forest.
Why it's worth a visit: This is not a park you visit expecting to be entertained. There are no programs to teach you about the outdoors, no playgrounds, no amenities beyond the very basics. But if you know about the outdoors and are just looking for a jumping-off point to do your own thing, this is the perfect place. The 85-mile Susquehannock Trail System bisects the park, so if you like to backpack, this is a great base camp. There is a mountain bike trail here as well.

56 Sizerville State Park

Location: North of Emporium
Season: Second Fri in Apr to mid-Dec
Sites: 23, some ADA accessible and some walk-in only
Maximum RV length: 40 feet
Facilities: Flush toilets, warm showers, water, electricity, sanitary dump station, play area, outdoor amphitheater
Fee per night: $$$-$$$$
Pets: Pets are allowed in 50 percent of the campsites.
Activities: Swimming, hiking, fishing, hunting, environmental education programs, annual Autumn Festival
Management: Pennsylvania Department of Conservation and Natural Resources
Contact: (814) 486-5605; www.dcnr.state.pa.us/stateparks/findapark/sizerville/index.htm. For reservations call toll-free (888) 727-2757 or visit VisitPaParks.com.
Finding the campground: From the junction of Routes 120 and 155 just east of Emporium, head north on Route 155 for about 7 miles. Turn right at the signs to enter the park.
GPS coordinates: N41 60.712' / W78 18.549'
Other: The reintroduction of beavers into Pennsylvania, following their overexploitation more than a century ago, began when a pair of animals donated to the state by Wisconsin were released in the park's East Branch Cowley Run in 1917. Today beavers are again widespread and abundant across Pennsylvania.
About the campground: This teardrop-shaped campground offers a good bit of space between sites. The walk-in ones adjacent to West Cowley Run are especially nice in spring and fall.
Why it's worth a visit: This park is a favorite of anglers who like fishing small mountain streams for trout. The east and west branches of Cowley Run are stocked with trout each spring and are known

to hold some wild trout as well, while Cowley Run offers freestone trout fishing at its best. Trout, as well as smallmouth bass, can also be caught in the branches of Sinnemahoning Creek.

There are some very nice hiking trails here of varied difficulty too. The 3-mile Sizerville Nature Trail, a loop path that offers relatively easy walking with interpretive markers all along the way, is especially nice.

If you want to try something special, the park hosts an Autumn Festival on the first Saturday of October. It offers food; all kinds of old-time crafts like candle making, quilting, and beekeeping; and make-it-and-take-it crafts as well.

57 Hills Creek State Park

Location: Northeast of Wellsboro
Season: Mid-Apr to late Oct
Sites: 80, some ADA accessible
Maximum RV length: 96 feet
Facilities: Flush toilets, warm showers, water, electricity, sanitary dump station, picnic tables, fire rings, coin-operated laundry, boat launch, some full-service sites
Fee per night: $$$–$$$$
Pets: Permitted at some sites
Activities: Boating (unpowered and electric motors only), swimming, hiking, fishing, environmental education programs
Management: Pennsylvania Department of Conservation and Natural Resources
Contact: (570) 724-4246; www.dcnr.state.pa.us/stateparks/findapark/hillscreek/index.htm. For reservations call toll-free (888) 727-2757 or visit VisitPaParks.com.
Finding the campground: From Wellsboro follow US 6/Route 660 east for about 6 miles. Turn left onto Whitneyville Road and go about 1.7 miles until you can turn right onto Hills Creek Lake Road. Go 1.3 mile and turn right onto Spillway Road.
GPS coordinates: N41 81.034'/W77 19.415'
Other: The park offers camping cottages, yurts, and 10 modern cabins for rent and an organized group tenting area.
About the campground: The campground is a series of connected loops.
Why it's worth a visit: This is another of those parks that's a small piece of woods tucked inside a much larger landscape. In this case, Hills Creek is a 407-acre park surrounded by about 13,000 acres of state land. There's plenty to do within the park itself though. The 137-acre lake is a nice draw. There's a beach for swimming and a snack bar and concession that are popular with families.

The waters are especially popular with anglers and boaters. Only electric motors are permitted, so easing around the shoreline on misty mornings is quiet, peaceful, and fun. There are fish to be caught—muskies, walleyes, bluegills, and largemouth bass, one of which holds the lake record of more than eight pounds—and wildlife to see. Waterfowl, ospreys, and even the occasional loon frequent the lake. Beavers are plentiful too. You can see their handiwork around the lake and throughout the park. The Lake Side Trail, a 3-mile path that begins near the campground, also offers good opportunities to see beavers, as well as lots of birds.

58 Tioga-Hammond Lakes Ives Run Campground

Location: Southwest of Tioga
Season: Mid-Apr through the end of Oct
Sites: 150, some walk-in only
Maximum RV length: 100 feet
Facilities: Flush toilets, warm showers, water, electricity, sanitary dump station, picnic tables, fire rings, boat launch and mooring
Fee per night: $$$–$$$$
Pets: Leashed pets permitted
Activities: Boating, swimming, hiking, fishing, hunting
Management: US Army Corps of Engineers, Baltimore District
Contact: (570) 835-5281; www.nab.usace.army.mil/Missions/Dams-Recreation/Tioga-Hammond/. For reservations call toll-free (877) 444-6777 or visit www.recreation.gov. There are some first-come, first-served campsites too.
Finding the campground: From Tioga follow Wellsboro Street/Route 287 east for 4.3 miles. Turn left onto Ives Run Road and go 1.3 miles and follow the signs to the campground.
GPS coordinates: N41 88.681'/W77 18.247'
Other: This park features two lakes: 685-acre Hammond Lake and 498-acre Tioga Lake. Of note to anglers, the state record crappie—4 pounds, 2.88 ounces—was caught from Hammond in 2000.
About the campground: Camping is located in the Ives Run area, in a couple of loops on Hammond Lake's south shore. There are waterfront sites as well as both shaded and open ones.
Why it's worth a visit: In addition to the boating, there's some interesting hiking here. The 9-mile C. Lynn Keller Trail offers some moderate, even difficult in places, hiking, but it's very scenic and even includes a pretty nice overlook. It's a footpath only; no bikes are allowed. Stephenhouse Trail is a 1.25-mile loop that offers tree identification information.

If you want to combine a hike with something extra, try Archery Trail—a 1-mile loop with sixteen archery targets and two tree stands set up at stations along the way. Bring your bow and you can get some exercise and practice your shooting along the way.

59 Cowanesque Lake Tompkins Campground

Location: North of Tioga
Season: Mid-May through the end of Sept
Sites: 86, some ADA accessible and some walk-in only
Maximum RV length: 68 feet
Facilities: Flush toilets, warm showers, water, electricity, sanitary dump station, picnic tables, fire rings, boat launch and mooring facilities
Fee per night: $$$–$$$$
Pets: Leashed pets permitted
Activities: Boating, swimming, hiking, fishing, hunting
Management: US Army Corps of Engineers, Baltimore District

Contact: (570) 835-5281; www.nab.usace.army.mil/Missions/Dams-Recreation/Cowanesque -Lake/. For reservations call toll-free (877) 444-6777 or visit www.recreation.gov. There are some first-come, first-served campsites too.

Finding the campground: From Tioga follow Route 287 north for 7.4 miles, crossing into New York. Turn left onto Bliss Road and follow it for about 4 miles until you see the signs for the campground.

GPS coordinates: N41 98.176' / W77 18.651'

Other: Boat launch facilities here can require a fee.

About the campground: This is a partially forested campground surrounded by a landscape that's equally a mixture of woods and fields.

Why it's worth a visit: This 1,085-acre lake with 17 miles of shoreline, located near the New York state line in north-central Pennsylvania, is popular with boaters and anglers. The lake is well-known for its tiger muskies and crappies, but anglers shouldn't overlook opportunities to cast a line at the north and south tailrace areas downstream of the dam.

Birders also spend a lot of time here. This facility is known as a hot spot for shorebird species such as semipalmated, least, solitary, and spotted sandpipers; dunlins; greater and lesser yel-lowlegs; black-bellied plovers; and killdeer. Bald eagles and ospreys nest here too. If you want to hike and look for some of those birds, Moccasin Trail is a 4-mile footpath that begins in the campground. The easy, fairly level walk follows the lake's northern shoreline and features rustic bridges, some nice benches, and scenic views of the lake.

Eastern Pennsylvania

Philadelphia to the Poconos

A cottontail rabbit pauses at the edge of a hedgerow at Hibernia Park.

Two cities—two big cities—one in Pennsylvania, one not, impact much of eastern Pennsylvania. The former is Philadelphia, the latter is New York City, which sends loads of people looking for open space in which to have fun into northeastern Pennsylvania each and every year.

The southern half of the region is dominated by Philadelphia, Pennsylvania's biggest metropolis and one of the largest in the country. Its reach extends beyond its own boundaries and into the counties around it, making this whole corner of the state one giant cluster of humanity. That means public campgrounds exist in a different form than elsewhere. There are several state parks, but only one, French Creek, offers camping; there are no federal campgrounds. Instead much of what's available is found in county parks that are smaller, more intimate oases amid the crowds.

It can be worth looking for those small nooks and crannies though because of the history to be explored. From the obvious such as the Liberty Bell and Independence Hall to the less-well-known Ninth Street Italian Market, you can walk and talk and shop the same Philadelphia streets once roamed by the likes of Benjamin Franklin, George Washington, and other revolutionaries. Speaking of Washington, Valley Forge National Historic Park is nearby. There are attractions of a more modern nature too, including Sesame Place, a park based on the *Sesame Street* television program.

North of Philadelphia, in the midsection of this region known as the Lehigh Valley, you'll find more fairly large cities—Easton, Bethlehem, and Allentown—as well as varied attractions, from the Museum of Indian Culture to the Crayola factory to some surprising bits of nature. There's some really outstanding whitewater to be run, as well as some fine fishing for trout and other species.

The northernmost portion of this region is the Poconos, the land of "endless mountains," and it seems it. While it's not as remote overall as the "Pennsylvania Wilds," you can certainly find breathtaking scenery.

You won't always enjoy it in solitude though. These forests serve as an outdoor playground for not only residents of Pennsylvania but New York City folks too. People drive from there—and elsewhere of course—to hike, bike, fish, and paddle. The Delaware River, the giant Lake Wallenpaupack, with its excellent fishing for a variety of species, and state parks like Ricketts Glen draw big crowds, especially on weekends. Ricketts Glen in particular can attract so many people at peak times that it actually has "overflow" parking lots, where you park and hike to the "real" parking lot so that you can hike some more to see its waterfalls.

Visiting Ricketts Glen is worth the effort though; that's true of the rest of this region too. You can check out natural oddities like the boulder field at Hickory Run State Park; visit the Pocono Environmental Educational Center at www.peec.org/, billed as the largest environmental education center in the Western Hemisphere; and wind up your day by touring Yuengling Brewery, America's oldest beer maker.

That's a lot to see and do, but that's what makes a visit worthwhile, right?

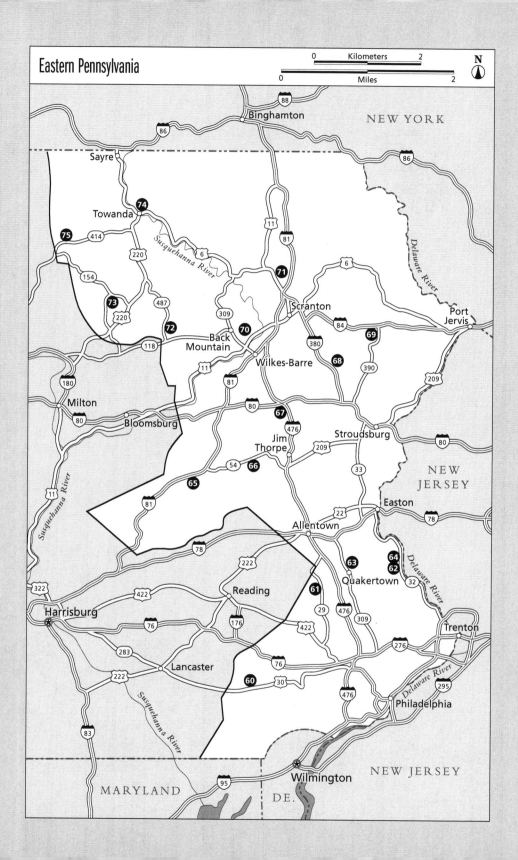

Park	Total Sites	Hookups	Max RV Length	Toilets	Showers	Drinking Water	Dump Station	Recreation	Fee	Reservation
60. Hibernia County Park	38	N	40	V	N	Y	Y	H, B, F, L, R, EE	$$–$$$	N
61. Green Lane Park	38	N	25	F	Y	Y	N	H, F, B, C, L, R, EE	$$$–$$$$	Y
62. Tohickon Valley Park	22	N	25	F	Y	Y	Y	H, S, F	$$–$$$	Y
63. Lake Towhee Park	17	N	25	F	N	Y	Y	H, B, F, EE	$$–$$$	Y
64. Tinicum Park	8	N/A	N/A	F	N	Y	N	H, B, F	$$–$$$	Y
65. Locust Lake State Park	282	Y	40	F	Y	Y	Y	H, B, F, S, C, EE, U	$$$–$$$$	Y
66. Mauch Chunk Lake Park	135	N	N/A	F	Y	Y	N	H, B, F, S, C, L, EE, U	$$–$$$$	Y
67. Hickory Run State Park	381	Y	40	F	Y	Y	Y	H, F, S, EE, U	$$$–$$$$	Y
68. Tobyhanna State Park	130	N	65	F	Y	Y	Y	H, B, F, S, C, U	$$$–$$$$	Y
69. Promised Land State Park	461	Y	75	F	Y	Y	Y	H, B, F, S, C, L, R, U	$$$–$$$$	Y
70. Frances Slocum State Park	97	Y	50	F	Y	Y	Y	H, B, F, S, C, L, U, EE	$$$–$$$$	Y
71. Lackawanna State Park	91	Y	40	F	Y	Y	Y	H, B, F, S, C, R, U, EE	$$$–$$$$	Y
72. Ricketts Glen State Park	120	Y	40	F	Y	Y	Y	H, B, F, S, L, R, EE, U	$$$–$$$$	Y
73. Worlds End State Park	70	Y	80	F	Y	Y	Y	H, B, F, EE, U	$$$–$$$$	Y
74. Larnard-Hornbrook County Park	40	Y	40	F	Y	Y	Y	H, F, L	$$$–$$$$	Y
75. Sunfish Pond County Park	50	Y	40	F	Y	Y	Y	H, B, F	$$$–$$$$	Y

Y = yes, N = no
Toilets: F = flush, V = vault
Recreation: H = hiking, B = boating, F = fishing, S = swimming, C = cycling, L = boat launch, R = horseback riding, EE = environmental education, U = hunting; O = off-road vehicle area.
Fee: $ to $$$$

60 Hibernia County Park

Location: North of Coatesville
Season: Mid-May to late Oct
Sites: 38, 19 in Fiddler's Campground and 19 in Lake Campground
Maximum RV length: 40 feet
Facilities: Vault toilets (though campers can use the flush toilets behind the park office), water, sanitary dump station, picnic table, fire ring, boat launch, volleyball court, playgrounds
Fee per night: $$–$$$
Pets: Leashed pets permitted
Activities: Boating (unpowered and electric motors only), hiking, horseback riding, fishing, environmental education programs
Management: Chester County
Contact: (610) 383-3812; www.chesco.org/ccparks. No reservations accepted most of the year; it's first come, first served except for the one weekend in August when the Old Fiddlers Picnic is held.
Finding the campground: From Coatesville follow Manor Road/Route 82 for 3.5 miles. Turn left onto Cedar Knoll Road; go 2 miles and turn left onto Park Road.
GPS coordinates: N40 03.313'/W75 83.592'
Other: Camping is permitted on Friday and Saturday nights only except for Memorial and Labor Day weekends, when you can also stay Sunday night.
About the campground: Fiddler's Campground is wooded and recommended for small RVs and pop-up trailers; Lake Campground is a mix of woods and open space and closer to the lake and its boat launch. There is no electricity at either campground.
Why it's worth a visit: This park's location alone makes it worthwhile, as southeastern Pennsylvania doesn't have a lot of public camping. A visit to Brandywine Creek is in order if you're an angler. It's only about 30 feet wide on average and less than 3 feet deep, but it gets stocked with trout and is pretty popular locally. The park is also home to 90-acre Chambers Lake, which holds warm-water species like bass and bluegills, and a tiny stocked pond that's open to children and the disabled during the first weeks of spring, then everyone after Memorial Day.

You'll also want to check out Hibernia Mansion, a nineteenth-century home that was once used by ironmasters and then a wealthy Philadelphia lawyer. It fell into disrepair after sitting vacant for fifteen years, but it has been restored and today is on the National Register of Historic Places. It's full of original period furniture and has been repainted to look as it did during its heyday. Tours are offered on weekends.

61 Green Lane Park

Location: Northeast of Pottstown
Season: Apr 1 to Nov 1
Sites: 30 in Deep Creek Campground, 8 in the equestrian campground
Maximum RV length: 25
Facilities: Flush toilets, warm showers, water, boat rentals, playgrounds, tennis courts

A swallowtail butterfly, half buried in a flower, provides a splash of color in Green Lane Park.

Fee per night: $$$-$$$$
Pets: Leashed pets permitted
Activities: Boating, hiking, mountain biking, horseback riding, fishing, movies and concerts, environmental education programs
Management: Montgomery County
Contact: Call (215) 234-4528 for information or reservations; https://montcopa.org/336/Parks.
Finding the campground: From Pottstown follow Route 663 North/North Charlotte Street for 3.6 miles. Turn right onto Route 663/Route 73 East/Big Red and go 2.1 miles. Turn left onto Snyder Road/Township Line Road and go 1 mile. Continue straight onto Little Road for 0.1 mile; continue straight on Snyder Road for 1.4 miles to the park.
GPS coordinates: N40 32.651'/W75 48.316' for Deep Creek; N40 33.796'/W75 48.530' for the equestrian campground
Other: There's no hunting here except for a special, permit-only goose hunt in September. There is a group camping area for nonprofits.
About the campground: Sites 1 through 8 are closest to the playground in Deep Creek Campground; sites 9 to 19 are closest to the restrooms and showers. The equestrian campground has two covered stalls.

Why it's worth a visit: This is big as county parks go, totaling more than 3,400 acres. There are three lakes: 814-acre Green Lane Reservoir, 38-acre Deep Creek Lake, and 26-acre Knight Lake. Green Lane Reservoir and Knight Lake contain largemouth bass, panfish, and catfish; Deep Creek Lake has all that plus stocked trout in spring, but only rented boats are permitted. If you're a birder, this park is listed as an "important bird area" for the variety of species that frequent here. The Church Road sanctuary is an especially good spot to visit with your binoculars.

Green Lane's public programs for families and nature camps run for children are really neat. Some of the latter are designed for kids in first through fifth grade; others are for slightly older children. All are designed to get kids outdoors and exploring. Public programs focus on everything from insects to aquatic animals to moss.

62 Tohickon Valley Park

Location: East of Quakertown, near Point Pleasant
Season: Year-round for sites 1 to 8; Apr 16 to Nov 14 for the rest
Sites: 22, some for tents only
Maximum RV length: 25 feet
Facilities: Flush toilets mid-Apr to Nov (vault toilets thereafter), warm showers, water, sanitary dump station, picnic tables, fire rings, swimming pool, playgrounds
Fee per night: $$–$$$
Pets: No pets allowed
Activities: Hiking, climbing, fishing
Management: Bucks County
Contact: (215) 297-0754 (in season); https://buckscounty.org/government/Parksand Recreation/Parks/Tohickon. For reservations call (215) 757-0751.
Finding the campground: From Quakertown head east on West Broad Street/Route 313 East for 10.2 miles. Turn left onto Stump Road and go 6.2 miles. Turn right onto Tohickon Hill Road and go 2.4 miles. Turn left onto Point Pleasant Pike, which almost immediately becomes River Road/Route 32. Continue 0.1 mile; take a slight left onto Cafferty Road and go 1.1 miles.
GPS coordinates: N40 43.785' / W75 07.636'
Other: This park also offers four cabins for rent in the Doe Run Campground.
About the campground: The Deer Wood Campground is often most crowded in late March and early November. For two days during each of those times, water pours out of nearby Lake Nocka-mixon at 500 feet per second, turning Tohickon Creek into a Class III and IV whitewater stream and drawing hordes of boaters. If you want to see them, check out the rapids near Cabin 4.
Why it's worth a visit: This 612-acre park is very near a number of big urban centers yet draws rock climbers from around the country. They come here to camp and climb the nearby 200-foot-tall red shale cliffs called High Rocks. The rocks are not within this park itself, although they are owned by Bucks County in part, in cooperation with Ralph Stover State Park. They were donated to the public by the famous author James Michener. Trails from the park lead to the cliffs, so this area is worth exploring even if you're not into rappelling. There is also some good primitive hiking through steeply sloping woods that border the boulder-filled Tohickon Creek gorge, as well as a spectacular vista.

Eighty-two species of birds, some of them rare, have been spotted here, as have copperheads, one of three venomous species of snake in Pennsylvania. Tohickon Creek is also a favorite with trout anglers.

63 Lake Towhee Park

Location: In Applebachsville, northeast of Quakertown
Season: Year-round
Sites: 17, some for tents only
Maximum RV length: 25 feet
Facilities: Flush toilets mid-Apr to Nov (vault toilets thereafter), water, sanitary dump station, fire rings, picnic tables, playground, ball field, nature area
Fee per night: $$–$$$
Pets: No pets allowed
Activities: Boating, hiking, fishing
Management: Bucks County

A young white-tailed deer casts a suspicious eye on visitors at Lake Towhee Park.

Contact: https://buckscounty.org/government/ParksandRecreation/Parks/Towhee. For reservations call (215) 757-0751.

Finding the campground: From Quakertown follow Route 313 east until you can turn left (north) onto West Thatcher Road. Go 0.3 mile; take the first left to stay on West Thatcher and go 1.8 miles. Turn right to stay on West Thatcher and go 1.3 miles. Turn left onto Old Bethlehem Road and go 1.1 miles. Follow the signs to the park.

GPS coordinates: N40 47.832' / W75 26.738'

Other: All of the amenities at this park are located on the western shore, so paddling to the eastern shoreline offers some real solitude.

About the campground: The campground is located on the park's western edge, near many of the day-use facilities.

Why it's worth a visit: This 549-acre park is home to 50-acre Lake Towhee, where you can fish for warmwater species like bass and panfish, tool around in a canoe or kayak, and take in some wildlife. Mallards, black ducks, Canada geese, and herons are numerous, as are assorted frogs and turtles. Exploring the nature area affords the opportunity to see white-tailed deer, squirrels, and a great number of songbirds.

Like the other parks in Bucks County offering camping, this one is also near Nockamixon State Park, which has a nearly 1,500-acre lake and other attractions but no camping outside of cabins. You can stay here and explore that bigger world, too.

64 Tinicum Park

Location: East of Quakertown, in Erwinna
Season: Year-round
Sites: 8, for tents only
Maximum RV length: N/A
Facilities: Flush toilets mid-Apr to Nov (vault toilets thereafter), water, picnic tables, fire rings, playground, disc golf, ball fields
Fee per night: $$–$$$
Pets: No pets allowed
Activities: Hiking, boating, fishing, environmental education programs
Management: Bucks County
Contact: https://buckscounty.org/government/ParksandRecreation/Parks/Tinicum. For reservations call (215) 757-0751.

Finding the campground: From Quakertown follow Route 313 east for 7.7 miles. Turn left onto Bedminster Road/Route 113 and go 6.1 miles. Continue another 0.3 mile after Bedminster/Route 113 becomes Hollow Horn Road. Turn right to stay on Hollow Horn and go less than 0.1 mile. Turn left to stay on the same road and go 1.2 miles. Make another right to stay on Hollow Horn; go 2.1 miles. Hollow Horn becomes Cafferty Road. Go 0.3 mile; turn right onto Hollow Horn and go 1.3 miles. Turn right onto Headquarters Road; go less than 0.1 mile. Stay straight on Tinicum Creek Road and go 0.8 mile. Turn left onto River Road/Route 32 and continue 1.7 miles to the park.

GPS coordinates: N40 50.969' / W75 06.911'

Other: This park hosts special events throughout the year: concerts by the Riverside Symphonia, an antiques show, and an art festival in July.

About the campground: The campground is located in a small wooded corner of the park, next to some large grass fields.

Why it's worth a visit: This 126-acre park sits practically on the Pennsylvania–New Jersey border and is near a number of historical attractions. The Delaware Canal and the Delaware River are on two sides of the park. The John Stover House, a restored Federal-style home dating to 1800, is here; tours are available on weekends from May through September. The park also hosts one of the largest kennel club dog shows in the country each May.

Perhaps the most unusual thing you could experience here are the polo matches hosted every Saturday from mid-May through September by the Tinicum Park Polo Club. The club has about four dozen players—including men and women from half a dozen countries—and hosts sanctioned events as well as club tournaments and family-friendly events such as Pooches and Polo, the Classic American Auto Show, the British Car Festival, and regular tailgate competitions. Visitors can watch, paying by the carload. You can even take polo lessons here.

65 Locust Lake State Park

Location: East of Frackville
Season: Mid-Mar to the third Sun in Oct
Sites: 282, some ADA accessible and some walk-in only in two campgrounds; tenting on the north side of the lake, tent and trailer camping on the south side
Maximum RV length: 40 feet
Facilities: Flush toilets, warm showers, water, electricity, sanitary dump station, picnic tables, fire rings, play areas, boat rental, camp store
Fee per night: $$$–$$$$
Pets: Permitted at some sites
Activities: Boating, swimming, hiking, biking on a paved trail, fishing, hunting, environmental education programs
Management: Pennsylvania Department of Conservation and Natural Resources
Contact: (570) 467-2404; www.dcnr.state.pa.us/stateparks/findapark/locustlake/index.htm. For reservations call toll-free (888) 727-2757 or visit VisitPaParks.com.
Finding the campground: From I-81 northbound, take exit 131B. Cross under the I-81 overpass and make an immediate left turn toward New Boston. Travel 1.1 miles to a marked left turn.
GPS coordinates: N40 78.438'/W76 12.049'
Other: A paved 1.3-mile bike trail encircles Locust Lake and provides some nice scenic views.
About the campground: All the sites in both campgrounds are wooded and within walking distance of the lake.
Why it's worth a visit: This park is a birder's delight. More than one hundred species have been documented within the park's boundaries, including sixteen species of birds of prey. The reason for the variety? The park lies within what's known as the Ridge and Valley Province of the Appalachian Plateau. Raptors follow those ridges, riding the updrafts they create, as they migrate south each fall. Common migrants include red-tailed and red-shouldered hawks and ospreys. Screech owls

A ranger drives to the entrance of the campground at Locust Lake State Park.

and great horned owls reside in the park year-round and can sometimes be seen and heard if you hike at dusk.

This is also a popular park in fall with hunters. Virtually the entire park is open to hunting. White-tailed deer, rabbits, squirrels, turkeys, and grouse are common species.

66 Mauch Chunk Lake Park

Location: West of Jim Thorpe
Season: Mid-Apr to the end of Oct
Sites: 135, all tents only
Maximum RV length: N/A
Facilities: Flush toilets, warm showers, water, picnic tables, fire rings, grill, boat rental, environmental education center, camp store
Fee per night: $$–$$$$
Pets: No pets allowed

Activities: Boating, swimming, hiking, biking, fishing, hunting, environmental education programs

Management: Carbon County

Contact: www.carboncounty.com/index.php/park. For reservations e-mail mauch2@ptd.net or call (570) 325-3669.

Finding the campground: From downtown Jim Thorpe head west on North Street/Route 903 for 0.6 mile. Turn left onto Route 209 and go 0.3 mile. Stay straight to continue on Broadway for another 1.4 miles. Broadway becomes Lentz Trail; follow it for 1.8 miles to the park.

GPS coordinates: N40 84.365'/W75 80.549'

Other: This is another huge county park, encompassing about 2,500 acres. It also has cottages and group camping sites for rent.

About the campground: All the sites are wooded; none have electricity.

Why it's worth a visit: Housed within the park is the Carbon County Environmental Education Center. Open year-round (free) in a former 1920s barn, it hosts a variety of public programs. Of particular note, it also serves as a wildlife rehabilitation center, with a number of live raptors on permanent display. As you walk the boardwalk trail, you can see a bald eagle, a golden eagle, screech and great horned owls, red-tailed and broad-winged hawks, an American kestrel, and other birds of prey. The center hosts a weeklong, overnight nature camp for children as well as a variety of public programs.

The 345-acre Mauch Chunk Lake holds bass, pickerel, panfish, and walleyes; Mauch Chunk Creek is stocked with trout each spring. The park loans fishing tackle free of charge. There are also some great hiking and biking trails. The Switchback Trail, the most popular, leads to Mount Pisgah and a magnificent overlook of Lehigh Gorge State Park.

67 Hickory Run State Park

Location: East of White Haven

Season: Modern facilities available the second Fri in Apr to the third Sun in Oct; rustic camping until Dec

Sites: 381 sites, some ADA accessible and some walk-in only

Maximum RV length: 40 feet

Facilities: Flush toilets, warm showers, water, electricity, sanitary dump station, picnic tables, fire rings, camp store, orienteering course, disc golf course

Fee per night: $$$-$$$$

Pets: Permitted at some sites

Activities: Swimming, hiking, orienteering, disc golf, fishing, hunting, environmental education programs

Management: Pennsylvania Department of Conservation and Natural Resources

Contact: (570) 443-0400; www.dcnr.state.pa.us/stateparks/findapark/hickoryrun/index.htm. For reservations call toll-free (888) 727-2757 or visit VisitPaParks.com.

Finding the campground: From I-80 near White Haven, take exit 274 (the Hickory Run State Park exit) onto Route 534 East. Make a slight right onto Route 534 and go 1.7 miles. Turn left to stay on Route 534 and go 3.3 miles to the park.

GPS coordinates: N41 02.386'/W75 68.945'

Glacially created Boulder Field is a striking National Natural Landmark in Hickory Run State Park.

Other: The park has 5 camping cottages. A visitor center complete with exhibits opened in October 2020. It will be located at the campground entrance. There's already a group tenting area.

About the campground: This is a large, industrial-scale campground that's too often frequented by black bears. The result is that all campers are required to store food and scented items, including toothpaste, deodorant, and dish soap, in their vehicle any time they leave the site, day or night, for even a short period of time.

Why it's worth a visit: There's a lot to do here, but you want to be sure to check out the Boulder Field, a National Natural Landmark. The 400 × 1,800-foot field of stone, up to 12 feet deep, is remarkable for its nearly complete lack of vegetation. This moonscape has sandstone boulders as big as 26 feet long. Why is it here, a striking open space surrounded by dense woods? Scientists say the boulders were carried off the surrounding ridges and dumped here by glaciers more than 20,000 years ago.

The park offers a GPS tour of the boulder field. Pick up a brochure at the park office and follow the coordinates to spots where you can hear Hickory Creek running under the rocks, see trees trying to infringe on the boulder field or some of the twelve species of snakes that live in the vicinity, or find the biggest boulders. Just be sure to treat the boulder field with care. Too many people try to take rocks home or paint on them; leave things as you found them. Park officials report that a continuing problem is people stacking the rocks into cairns that have to be disassembled so that the next visitors can experience the park in its natural state.

When you're done with the boulder field, explore some of what else this park has to offer, including 44 miles of hiking trails, stream fishing for trout, disc golf, and hunting for big and small game.

68 Tobyhanna State Park

Location: North of Tobyhanna
Season: Second Fri in Apr to third Sun in Oct
Sites: 130, some ADA accessible
Maximum RV length: 65 feet
Facilities: Flush toilets, hot showers, water, sanitary dump station, picnic tables, fire rings, playground
Fee per night: $$$–$$$$
Pets: Permitted at some sites
Activities: Boating, swimming, hiking, mountain biking, fishing, hunting
Management: Pennsylvania Department of Conservation and Natural Resources
Contact: (570) 894-8336; www.dcnr.state.pa.us/stateparks/findapark/tobyhanna/index.htm. For reservations call toll-free (888) 727-2757 or visit VisitPaParks.com.
Finding the campground: From Tobyhanna follow Route 423 north for about 2.4 miles. Turn left at the signs into the park.
GPS coordinates: N41 21.089' / W75 39.906'
Other: Be on the lookout for old, unexploded artillery shells. This area was once the artillery-training center for West Point cadets. Three kinds of shells, from 3 to 24 inches long, have been found in some of the least-used, more-remote parts of the park. If you come across one, leave it untouched and contact the park office.
About the campground: This campground, located at an elevation of about 2,000 feet, which is fairly high for Pennsylvania, is shaped sort of like a V, with the right arm being the pet area and closer to Tobyhanna Lake. There's also an organized group tenting area.
Why it's worth a visit: If you like to challenge yourself while hiking, this is the place. The park doesn't have a ton of trails—there are 10 miles all told—but at least half of what it does have is of the very rugged variety. The scenery can be worth it though.

The 3.3-mile Yellow Trail in particular is worth the effort. You'll have to do some rock hopping and negotiate a few wet areas, but the trail cuts through the 1,600-acre Black Bear/Bender Swamp, a state-designated natural area. Here you can see carnivorous plants such as the pitcher plant and yellow bladderwort and in July fields of blueberries, which also attract black bears. The Lake Trail is a paved bike trail that also passes the natural area, although to a much lesser degree.

Make some time to fish or float 170-acre Tobyhanna Lake. This quiet, electric-motor-only lake has its share of brook trout, bass, pickerel, and yellow perch.

69 Promised Land State Park

Location: North of Canadensis

Season: Pickerel Point and Beechwood, Apr to Oct, weather permitting; Northwoods, Hemlock Hills, Equestrian Campground, Pines, Rhododendron and Deerfield, May to Oct

Sites: 275 modern sites, 186 rustic sites, some ADA accessible and some walk-in only

Maximum RV length: 75 feet at Deerfield Campground, 65 feet at Pickerel Point, 40 feet at Pines Campground

Facilities: Flush and vault toilets (depending on campground), showers (for a fee at Pines Campground, free everywhere else), full-service sites, water, electricity, sanitary dump station, picnic tables, fire rings, boat rental, orienteering courses

Fee per night: $$$–$$$$

Pets: Permitted at some sites

Activities: Boating, swimming, hiking, orienteering, mountain and road biking, horseback riding, fishing, hunting, environmental education programs

Management: Pennsylvania Department of Conservation and Natural Resources

Contact: (570) 676-3428; www.dcnr.state.pa.us/stateparks/findapark/promisedland/index.htm. For reservations call toll-free (888) 727-2757 or visit VisitPaParks.com.

Finding the campground: From Canadensis go north on Route 390 for 10 miles. Going left at the park office will take you to the Lower Lake Campground; going right leads to Pickerel Point and Deerfield Campgrounds; continuing straight on Route 390 leads to the Pines Campground.

GPS coordinates: N41 31.801'/W75 22.991' for Lower Lake; N41 30.272'/W75 19.361' for Pickerel Point/Deerfield; N41 32.125'/W75 20.416' for Pines

Other: Pickerel Point and Deerfield Campgrounds were renovated and reopened in mid-2012. The park also offers rustic cabins for rent.

About the campgrounds: Lower Lake Campground (the collective name for the Beechwood, Northwoods, Rhododendron, and Hemlock HIlls areas) is the biggest. Pines Campground is much smaller and a little more open. Pickerel Point is on a spit of land extending into Promised Land Lake and provides larger sites with more space between them on the shoreline; adjacent Deerfield is a loop with primitive amenities. Pickerel Point also features full-service electric, water, and sewage hookups; that's a first for the state park system.

Why it's worth a visit: There are a lot of woods here. Promised Land comprises 3,000 acres and is surrounded by more than 12,000 acres of Delaware State Forest. That means lots to do, both on water and on land. Look at a map and you'll see that Promised Land State Park features two lakes, which are all but connected by a stream near the park's main day-use area. There are two swimming beaches and warmwater fishing in Promised Land Lake and trout fishing in Lower Lake. While on the latter, be sure to look for the bald eagle nest that's visible from a wildlife observation deck near Bear Wallow boat launch. Both lakes are open to unpowered craft and those with electric motors only, so there are opportunities for quiet fishing and cruising.

Keep an eye out for black bears, which are a common sight here. Mid-June to mid-July, when the mountain laurel is in full bloom, is a good time to be at this park.

70 Frances Slocum State Park

Location: North of Wilkes-Barre
Season: Second Fri in Apr to third Sat in Oct
Sites: 97, some ADA accessible and 15 walk-in only
Maximum RV length: 50 feet
Facilities: Flush toilets, warm showers, water, electricity, sanitary dump station, picnic table, fire ring, boat launch, seasonal camp store, nature center
Fee per night: $$$-$$$$
Pets: Permitted at some sites
Activities: Boating, swimming, hiking, mountain biking, fishing, hunting, environmental education programs
Management: Pennsylvania Department of Conservation and Natural Resources
Contact: (570) 696-3525; www.dcnr.state.pa.us/stateparks/findapark/francesslocum/index .htm. For reservations call toll-free (888) 727-2757 or visit VisitPaParks.com.

A cardinal takes off from a split-rail fence at the bird-feeding station at Frances Slocum State Park.

Finding the campground: From Wilkes-Barre merge onto Route 309 north for 5.7 miles. Turn right (east) onto Caverton Road and go 4.2 miles. Turn left (north) onto West Eighth Street and drive 1.3 miles. Turn left (west) onto Mt. Oliver Road and go 1 mile to the park entrance on the left.
GPS coordinates: N41 33.591'/W75 88.394'

Other: This park was named for a 5-year-old girl who was taken from her Quaker parents by Delaware Indians. She tried to escape that first night, was recaptured, and spent decades living with the tribe, refusing to come home when learning her real name at age 62. You can hike the 0.7-mile Frances Slocum Trail to see the rock shelter where she was hidden during her first night of captivity.

About the campground: This is a lot of campsites crammed into a small space, so expect neighbors—lots of them. There's also an organized group tenting area.

Why it's worth a visit: Horseshoe-shaped Frances Slocum Lake is the main attraction here. The 165-acre lake is open to canoes, kayaks, and motorboats with electric motors, and you can bring your own or rent one here. While you're on the water, you can fish for a variety of warmwater species, including bass and abundant walleyes, which are stocked in the lake. There are good numbers of black crappies too and, for the kids, bluegills and pumpkinseeds. You can also explore the lake's edges looking for frogs, turtles, and insects.

Away from the water, mountain bikers have 4 miles of red-blazed trails of varying difficulty in the western edge of the park; hikers have 13 miles of trails. The 3.2-mile Deer Trail, which starts at the nature center and winds through a variety of habitats, is a popular one, as is the 1.4-mile Lakeshore Trail, which is popular with anglers. Bird feeding and butterfly gardens offer places to spend some quiet time.

71 Lackawanna State Park

Location: North of Scranton
Season: Mid-Apr to mid-Oct
Sites: 91, some ADA accessible and some walk-in only
Maximum RV length: 40 feet
Facilities: Flush toilets, warm showers, water, electricity, sanitary dump station, picnic tables, fire rings, pool, boat rental
Fee per night: $$$-$$$$
Pets: Permitted at some sites
Activities: Boating, swimming, hiking, mountain biking, horseback riding, fishing, hunting, environmental education programs
Management: Pennsylvania Department of Conservation and Natural Resources
Contact: (570) 945-3239; www.dcnr.state.pa.us/stateparks/findapark/lackawanna/index.htm. For reservations call toll-free (888) 727-2757 or visit VisitPaParks.com.
Finding the campground: From Scranton follow I-81 north for about 8 miles. Take exit 199 and travel 3 miles west on Route 524 to the park.
GPS coordinates: N41 55.933'/W75 71.563'
Other: The campground has cottages and yurts for rent and has an organized group camping area.
About the campground: The campground consists of multiple loops. A scenic overlook separates the Maple Lane and Fox Run loops. All sites are within relative walking distance of the pool and lake.

Why it's worth a visit: The park is just packed with multiuse trails open to hiking, mountain biking, and horseback riding. There are 18 miles of hiking trails—all of them interconnected loops so that you can plan your walk to be as long or as short as you'd like—and 15 miles of biking and equestrian trail. Many of those biking/equestrian trails are on the side of the park opposite the campground, but it's possible to work your way there without having to use your vehicle.

The other big draw at this park is 198-acre, 2.5-mile-long Lackawanna Lake. No gas motors are allowed, so it's very popular with canoers, kayakers, rowers, and those with sailboats. The park rents boats and even conducts a number of learn-to-kayak and learn-to-paddle classes to meet the demand for public access to the lake. Anglers who take to the lake can find good fishing for trout, muskies, walleyes, catfish, and panfish.

72 Ricketts Glen State Park

Location: West of Wilkes-Barre
Season: 12 months
Sites: 120, some walk-in only and some ADA accessible
Maximum RV length: 40 feet
Facilities: Flush toilets, warm showers, water, electricity, sanitary dump station, picnic tables, fire rings, boat rental
Fee per night: $$$–$$$$
Pets: Permitted at some sites
Activities: Boating, swimming, hiking, horseback riding, fishing, hunting, environmental education programs
Management: Pennsylvania Department of Conservation and Natural Resources
Contact: (570) 477-5675; www.dcnr.state.pa.us/stateparks/findapark/rickettsglen/index.htm. For reservations call toll-free (888) 727-2757 or visit VisitPaParks.com.
Finding the campground: From I-81 in Wilkes-Barre, take Route 309 north toward Kingston. Route 309 becomes Memorial Highway/Route 415. Continue for 2.2 miles and turn left (south) onto Route 118. Go 17.7 miles; turn right (north) onto Red Rock Mountain Road/Route 487 and go 3.7 miles. Note that the section of Route 487 from the town of Red Rock to the Lake Jean area of the park is a very steep road. Heavy trailer units should avoid this hill and enter the park by taking Route 487 south from Dushore.
GPS coordinates: N41 33.648'/W76 29.584'
Other: The park has 10 modern cabins for rent, deluxe camping cottages, and 5 organized group tenting areas, each of which can accommodate 40 people. There is a nonrefundable transaction fee charged on all overnight and day-use reservations.
About the campground: All campers must stop at the park office to pick up their permit and park guidelines prior to going to the campground. The campground has two loops, the larger one fronting Lake Jean.
Why it's worth a visit: If there are a handful of must-see parks in Pennsylvania, Ricketts Glen is one of them. And the park is famous for one thing above all else: its waterfalls. The park's Glens Natural Area, a National Natural Landmark, is home to twenty-two named waterfalls ranging in height from 11 to 94 feet. All are spectacular. Quite simply, this is a gorgeous place to do some hiking. It's not easy, though.

Hikers cool off under 94-foot Ganoga Falls, the tallest of twenty-two named waterfalls within Ricketts Glen State Park.

Seeing all the falls requires walking the 7.2-mile Falls Trail. You can see nineteen of them by taking a 3.2-mile loop, but even that shorter trek will challenge you. You descend into the valley from the get-go and climb your way back out on trails that are narrow and full of rock steps. Imagine going down and up a tall building's worth of stairs and you get the idea. But the effort is worth it; the falls are absolutely stunning. The 94-foot Ganoga Falls is especially popular—people walk beneath it to cool off. Just don't expect to enjoy much solitude here, especially if you come on a weekend. The falls draw crowds so large that you're often forced to park your vehicle in one of a couple overflow lots and walk just to reach the trailhead. Once you've seen the falls, spend some time exploring the rest of the park. The 245-acre Lake Jean is fun to paddle, and it has a swimming beach that lets you cool off after hiking to see the falls.

73 Worlds End State Park

Location: South of Towanda
Season: Mid-Apr to the first week of Dec
Sites: 70, some ADA accessible and some walk-in only
Maximum RV length: 80 feet
Facilities: Flush toilets, warm showers, water, electricity at some sites, sanitary dump station, picnic tables, fire rings, four scenic overlooks
Fee per night: $$$–$$$$
Pets: Permitted at some sites
Activities: Swimming, whitewater rafting, hiking, fishing, hunting, environmental education programs
Management: Pennsylvania Department of Conservation and Natural Resources
Contact: (570) 924-3287; www.dcnr.state.pa.us/stateparks/findapark/worldsend/index.htm. For reservations call toll-free (888) 727-2757 or visit VisitPaParks.com.
Finding the campground: From Towanda follow US 220 south for 18 miles. Turn right (west) onto Route 87 and go 12 miles. Turn left (south) onto Route 154 and go 1.7 miles to the park.
GPS coordinates: N41 46.680' / W76 57.205'
Other: The park has 19 rustic cabins for rent as well as a rustic organized group camping area.
About the campground: The campground consists of two loops. The nonelectric sites, the walk-in sites in particular, have more space.
Why it's worth a visit: Located along the banks of S-shaped Loyalsock Creek in a narrow valley, this park gets attention from whitewater rafters March through May, when water levels are sufficient to offer some fun. Later in the year—especially during the June mountain laurel bloom and the peak of the fall foliage season in October—there are several overlooks worth visiting: Loyalsock Canyon, Worlds End, High Rock or High Knob, and Butternut. The overlooks are accessed via narrow dirt and gravel roads. The roads get no maintenance in winter and can be well groomed or rough, depending on when you are there, but the views at the end are worth it.

You can also leave the car behind and take some of the park's 20 miles of hiking trails. They are, as you would expect, often steep and rocky. But you get to see some things most people don't. The 1.2-mile Double Run Natural Trail can be steep in places but passes by lots of wildflowers in spring, along with waterfalls and pools. The 3.25-mile Worlds End Trail takes you to Worlds End Vista and crosses Pioneer Road, where travelers more than a century ago reportedly gave the area its name after seeing the steep drop to the river below. And be sure to visit the Rock Garden, just upslope from Loyalsock Canyon Vista. It's a blocky maze of rock perfect for exploring.

74 Larnard-Hornbrook County Park

Location: North of Towanda
Season: Early May through mid-Oct
Sites: 40
Maximum RV length: 40 feet
Facilities: Flush toilets, showers, water, electricity, sanitary dump station, softball field, volleyball courts, horseshoe pits, boat launch
Fee per night: $$$–$$$$
Pets: Leashed pets permitted
Activities: Boating, fishing
Management: Bradford County
Contact: (570) 265-1719; https://bradfordcountypa.org/county-parks/
Finding the campground: From Towanda follow Sheshequin Road/Route 1043 north for 4 miles. Turn left onto Hornbrook Park Road/Route 1045 and go 1 mile to the park.
GPS coordinates: N41 81.744' / W76 49.686'
Other: The park comprises about 30 acres; a little less than half that acreage is an island in the Susquehanna River.
About the campground: Campsites are largely in the open, on the edge of tree lines and hedgerows. Daily, weekly, monthly, and seasonal camping is available.
Why it's worth a visit: This park draws a lot of seasonal campers, who stay the entire summer. The main draw is the North Branch Susquehanna River, which for years has been considered one of, if not the, best smallmouth bass fisheries east of the Mississippi. Ongoing concerns with rising water temperatures farther downstream have tempered that assessment in recent years, but the fishing remains excellent in this stretch. Even if you leave your rod at home, jumping in a canoe or kayak gives you the chance to see all kinds of wildlife, including bald eagles.

If you want to visit somewhere interesting nearby, check out the French Azilum Historic Site in nearby Towanda. The colony was populated by French loyalists who fled that country's revolution in the late 1700s. They stayed until Emperor Napoleon Bonaparte granted immunity and allowed them to return without facing the guillotine. Today visitors can check out structures remaining from the colony and learn about life at that time. For information visit https://thefrenchazilum.com/.

75 Sunfish Pond County Park

Location: East of Canton
Season: Early May through mid-Oct
Sites: 50, 12 of them tent-only
Maximum RV length: 40 feet

A dragonfly with iridescent wings perches on the stem of a water plant on the shores of Sunfish Pond.

Facilities: Flush toilets, showers, water, electricity, sanitary dump station, camp store that also sells some prepared food

Fee per night: $$$–$$$$

Pets: Leashed pets permitted

Activities: Boating, hiking, fishing

Management: Bradford County

Contact: (570) 265-1719; https://bradfordcountypa.org/county-parks/

Finding the campground: Sunfish Pond County Park is in LeRoy Township, adjacent to State Game Land 12. From Towanda take Route 414 west. Turn left on State Rte 3010 in the town of Leroy. Signs direct you to Sunfish Pond; follow this road straight through the next intersection and continue up Leroy Mountain Road to the top of the mountain, where you will see a right turn and sign pointing to Sunfish Pond.

GPS coordinates: N41 64.34' / W76 69.66'

Other: This park was the site of the first state-managed wild game refuge established on private land. A "refuge keeper" lived here from the early 1900s through 1946 to kill vermin, fight fires, plant trees, and raise game species.

About the campground: The campground offers a mix of sites—some shaded, some on the edges of tree lines. It also reopens for the state's two-week deer hunting season in early December. Daily, weekly, monthly, and seasonal camping is available.

Why it's worth a visit: This park, as you can tell by the directions to get here, is on top of a rugged mountain in an out-of-the-way location. That means it's very peaceful and tranquil, if potentially difficult to get to. But people have been coming here for generations. Originally known as Crystal Lake, this pond has been drawing tourists for more than a century. It was shut off to the public as a park starting in 1915 when the game refuge was established here, but a land swap in the early 1970s paved the way for the park's creation. Today Sunfish Pond offers good fishing for stocked trout in spring and warmwater fishing for bass, catfish, and panfish throughout summer. The park is just 70 acres, but it's surrounded by 50,000 acres of state land, so there's plenty of space for hiking or riding a mountain bike.

Southern Pennsylvania

Ridges to Fields

Water spills over the dam below Greenwood Lake, where visitors can boat, swim, and fish.

Picture an accordion. One part is all ridges, grooves folded up tightly against one another. The other part, the keyboard, is broad, flat, not totally without features but hardly rough. That's southern Pennsylvania.

The western part of this region is known as the Allegheny Front. Part of the eastern continental divide, this is the grooved portion of the accordion, with countless narrow ridges folded one against another, separated by fertile if relatively skinny valleys. Boasting elevations of about 3,000 feet at their highest point, these ridges gradually fall away to flat, rich, wide farm country—the state's breadbasket, so to speak—that's closer to 340 feet above sea level. That's the region's eastern part, the keyboard. Together they have been said to look like corduroy from the air.

Visitors can find a lot to see and do in this region's two areas.

Outdoor options are plentiful. Birds of all sorts love the ridges. They're natural migration corridors, so all manner of large raptors ride their air currents south in big numbers each fall, drawing flocks of binocular-wielding birders. There's some great paddling in this area too. The Susquehanna and Juniata River water trails offer great Class I paddling, as do the Raystown and Frankstown Branches, if more seasonally. And of course there's Raystown Lake—a 28-mile-long Army Corps of Engineers impoundment that attracts powerboaters like a magnet draws metal filings. The lake is home to huge striped bass, and the park offers bald eagles, a two-story visitor center, and some terrific hiking, as well as some boat-in camping.

Want to sample some sweets? Nearby is State College, surrounding Penn State University, which is famous not only for its football team but also for the fresh-made ice cream of the Berkey Creamery. Hersheypark, the amusement park in the town named for Milton Hershey and his iconic chocolate bar, is located here as well.

If it's history you prefer, there's the Horseshoe Curve, a nearly 0.75-mile-long stretch of railroad that curves back on itself more than 180 degrees, and the Railroaders Memorial Museum. The Johnstown Flood Museum—which explores the tragedy that cost more than 2,200 people their lives—and Johnstown Incline are nearby. Downtown Harrisburg is home to the National Civil War Museum. That's fitting because this is also the part of the state where you find Gettysburg, where the Confederacy entered Pennsylvania—in what was its high-water mark for northern invasion—for an epic three-day battle.

And for something totally different, there's what's known as Pennsylvania's Dutch Country for its concentration of Amish. You can explore that culture at the Amish Village, a one-stop shop of all things Old World.

With all that's available in the region, the question is not if there's anything to do but how to squeeze it all in. Have a good time finding your answer!

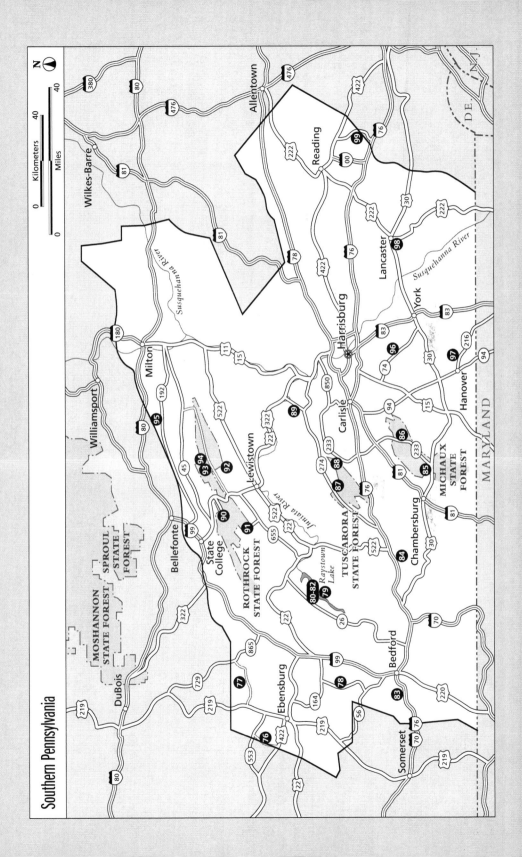

Park	Total Sites	Hookups	Max RV Length	Toilets	Showers	Drinking Water	Dump Station	Recreation	Fee	Reservation
76. Duman Lake County Park	6	Y	40	F	Y	Y	Y	H, B, F, L, EE	$$$–$$$$	Y
77. Prince Gallitzin State Park	398	Y	40	F	Y	Y	Y	H, B, F, S, C, L, R, EE, U	$$$–$$$$	Y
78. Blue Knob State Park	48	Y	40	F	Y	Y	Y	H, F, C, R, E, U	$$$–$$$$	Y
79. Trough Creek State Park	29	Y	40	V	N	Y	Y	H, F, U	$$$–$$$$	Y
80. Raystown Lake Susquehannock Campground	61	N	75	V	N	Y	N	H, B, F, S, C, U	$$–$$$	Y
81. Raystown Lake Seven Points Campground	261	Y	75	F	Y	Y	Y	H, B, F, S, C, L, EE, U	$$$$	Y
82. Raystown Lake Nancy's Campground	50	N/A	N/A	V	N	N	N	H, B, F, U	$–$$	N
83. Shawnee State Park	212	Y	45	F	Y	Y	Y	H, B, F, S, C, L, EE, U	$$$–$$$$	Y
84. Cowans Gap State Park	201	Y	40	F	Y	Y	Y	H, B, F, S, U, EE	$$$–$$$$	Y
85. Caledonia State Park	175	Y	60	F	Y	Y	Y	H, F, S, EE, U	$$$–$$$$	Y
86. Pine Grove Furnace State Park	70	Y	60	F	Y	Y	Y	H, B, F, S, C, L, EE, U	$$$–$$$$	Y
87. Fowlers Hollow State Park	17	Y	50	F	N	Y	Y	H, F, C, R, U	$$$–$$$$	Y
88. Colonel Denning State Park	49	N	40	V	N	Y	Y	H, B, F, S, U	$$$–$$$$	Y
89. Little Buffalo State Park	45	Y	55	F	Y	Y	Y	H, B, F, S, L, EE, U	$$$–$$$$	Y
90. Penn-Roosevelt State Park	18	N	N/A	V	N	Y	N	H, R, U	$$–$$$$	N
91. Greenwood Furnace State Park	48	Y	40	F	Y	Y	Y	H, B, F, S, L, EE, U	$$$–$$$$	Y
92. Reeds Gap State Park	14	N	N/A	V	Y	Y	N	H, F, EE, U	$$$–$$$$	Y
93. Poe Valley State Park	45	Y	40	F	Y	Y	Y	H, F, B, S, EE	$$$–$$$$	Y
94. Poe Paddy State Park	36	N	40	V	Y	Y	Y	H, F	$$$–$$$$	Y
95. Raymond B. Winter State Park	61	Y	40	F	Y	Y	Y	H, F, S, C, EE, U	$$$–$$$$	Y
96. Gifford Pinchot State Park	284	Y	95	F	Y	Y	Y	H, B, F, S, C, R, EE, U	$$$–$$$$	Y
97. Codorus State Park	193	Y	54	F	Y	Y	Y	H, B, F, S, R, EE, U	$$$–$$$$	Y
98. Lancaster County Central Park	5	N	N/A	V	N	Y	N	H, B, F, C, EE, S	$$$–$$$$	Y
99. French Creek State Park	199	Y	50	F	Y	Y	Y	H, B, F, S, C, L, R, EE, U	$$$–$$$$	Y

Y = yes, N = no
Toilets: F = flush, V = vault
Recreation: H = hiking, B = boating, F = fishing, S = swimming, C = cycling, L = boat launch, R = horseback riding, EE = environmental education, U = hunting; O = off-road vehicle area.
Fee: $ to $$$$

76 Duman Lake County Park

Location: Northwest of Ebensburg
Season: Mid-Apr to mid-Nov
Sites: 6 (The park sometimes works with campers to create additional sites as needed.)
Maximum RV length: 40 feet
Facilities: Flush toilets, warm showers, water, electricity, sanitary dump station, picnic tables, fire ring, playground, horseshoe pits, softball fields, volleyball and basketball courts, exercise trail, miniature train, camp store
Fee per night: $$$-$$$$
Pets: Leashed pets permitted
Activities: Boating (unpowered and electric motors only), hiking, fishing, environmental education programs, train and hayrides
Management: Cambria County
Contact: www.cambriacountypa.gov/duman-park.aspx. For reservations call (814) 472-8514.

A gray squirrel pauses while scampering down a tree at Duman Lake County Park, which operates one of the smallest public campgrounds in the state.

Finding the campground: From Ebensburg head west to cross US 219 and follow Benjamin Franklin Highway for 6.5 miles. Continue for another 1.3 miles after Benjamin Franklin Highway becomes US 422. Turn right (north) onto Route 271/Duman Road and go 4.3 miles. Turn right onto County Park Road and go 0.9 mile to the park.

GPS coordinates: N40 56.799'/W78 84.204'

Other: The park hosts a number of dog shows throughout the year.

About the campground: Unreserved sites are available on a first-come, first-served basis.

Why it's worth a visit: This is Cambria County's only park, and it's a small one—71 acres overall, including a 19-acre lake. The campground is, not surprisingly, run sort of like a mom-and-pop operation, but in a good way. There are just six official sites, but if they're full, a call to the county can often get you set up in a spot that can handle your needs.

Given the variety of things to do, this is a nice park to take kids camping, especially if it's their first outing. For anglers the lake is stocked with trout several times a year and also holds bass and bluegills, if small ones. The park also has ball fields, horseshoe courts, an exercise trail, and a playground. Small children especially will like the miniature train rides and hayrides that are offered throughout the summer season.

77 Prince Gallitzin State Park

Location: Northwest of Altoona

Season: 7 months; second Fri in Apr to last Mon in Oct

Sites: 398, some ADA accessible

Maximum RV length: 40 feet

Facilities: Flush toilets, warm showers, water, electricity, sanitary dump stations, picnic tables, fire rings, playgrounds, boat rentals, boat mooring, camp store with coin-operated laundry

Fee per night: $$$–$$$$

Pets: Permitted at some sites

Activities: Boating, swimming, hiking, road biking and mountain biking, horseback riding, fishing, hunting, environmental education programs

Management: Pennsylvania Department of Conservation and Natural Resources

Contact: (814) 674-1000; www.dcnr.state.pa.us/stateparks/findapark/princegallitzin/index.htm. For reservations call toll-free (888) 727-2757 or visit VisitPaParks.com.

Finding the campground: From Altoona follow Route 36 west for 9.3 miles. Turn right onto Route 53 north; go 7.8 miles and turn left onto State Park Road. After 0.2 mile State Park Road becomes Marina Road. Continue another 2.8 miles to the park.

GPS coordinates: N40 67.457'/W78 56.933'

Other: The park has camping cottages and modern cabins for rent and has an organized group tenting area.

About the campground: Pets are permitted in the Red Oak and Beech loops. ADA-accessible sites are scattered throughout this large campground.

Why it's worth a visit: You know those projects around home that start out as something little and then blossom into something much bigger? That's Prince Gallitzin State Park. In 1955 the local chamber of commerce and sportsmen proposed building a 30-acre lake in this area to boost the local economy and give outdoorsmen a place to go. Two years later, when work to develop the park

Prince Gallitzin is home to a variety of songbirds, like this eastern bluebird.

began, the plans called for a 1,760-acre lake as the centerpiece of "Pennsylvania's largest and most complete state park." That's just about what Prince Gallitzin is today.

At 1,635 acres the lake's a tad smaller than planned, but it's a real draw for sportsmen. It offers excellent fishing for bass, northern pike, crappies, yellow perch, and even bowfin—a prehistoric species found in only a handful of waters within the state. Boaters love the lake too. You'll see sailboats riding the wind, pontoon boats cruising the lake's bays, and kayaks following the shores. Boats are available for rent if you don't have your own; lake tours are offered as well.

Away from the water there are more than 32 miles of trails for hiking and/or biking. The 2.2-mile Campground Trail follows the lakeshore and has benches scattered along the way so that you can stop, relax, and take in views of the lake.

78 Blue Knob State Park

Location: North of Bedford
Season: Second Fri in Apr to third Sat in Oct
Sites: 48, some ADA accessible and 2 walk-in only

Flowers greet visitors to Blue Knob State Park in Bedford County.

Maximum RV length: 40 feet
Facilities: Flush toilets, warm showers, water, electricity, sanitary dump station, picnic tables, fire rings, playground
Fee per night: $$$–$$$$
Pets: Permitted at some sites
Activities: Swimming, hiking, mountain biking, horseback riding, fishing, hunting, environmental education programs
Management: Pennsylvania Department of Conservation and Natural Resources
Contact: (814) 276-3576; www.dcnr.state.pa.us/stateparks/findapark/blueknob/index.htm. For reservations call toll-free (888) 727-2757 or visit VisitPaParks.com.
Finding the campground: From the east or west, take the Pennsylvania Turnpike (I-76) to Bedford, exit 146. From Bedford go north on I-99/US 220 for 6.6 miles toward Altoona. Take exit 7 toward St. Clairsville/Osterburg and go 0.3 mile. Turn left onto Route 869/Brunbaugh Road and go 0.2 mile. Turn right onto Route 869/William Penn Road and go 1.5 miles. Turn left onto Route 869/Heritage Road; go 0.3 mile and turn left to stay on Route 869/Heritage Road. Go 4.1 miles; turn right onto Route 869/Burnt House Road and go 3.7 miles. Turn right onto Church Road and go 0.1 mile. Turn left, go 2.8 miles, and take a slight right onto Forrest Road. Go 0.7 mile and take the first right onto Ski Access Road. Continue 0.6 mile to the park.
GPS coordinates: N40 28.948'/W78 58.932'
Other: The park offers three modern cabins and one house for rent.
About the campground: The campground comprises two loops. Sites on the outsides of the loops are the most spacious.
Why it's worth a visit: Blue Knob is best known for its downhill skiing in winter. It is, after all, home to the second-tallest mountain in the state, one that stands just 67 feet lower than Mount Davis in nearby Somerset County. But it's also a great place to hike in warmer weather, especially if you like scenic views. There are four of note here: a southeastern view from the Chappells Field area across from the campground; a southern view from the Willow Spring picnic area; a southwestern view from Mountain View Trail; and a northeastern view from the Expressway chairlift on land leased by the ski resort.

There are 18 miles of hiking trails—not counting a 26-mile backpacking trail that passes through the park—ranging from easy, kid-friendly ones to others that will test your stamina. There's some really good fishing to be had for stocked and wild trout as well. Mountain bikers also visit here, with three trails in particular—Crist Ridge, Rock 'N' Ridge, and Mountain View—open to expert bikers.

79 Trough Creek State Park

Location: South of Huntingdon
Season: Mid-Apr through mid-Dec
Sites: 29, some ADA accessible and some walk-in only
Maximum RV length: 40 feet
Facilities: Vault toilets, water, sanitary dump station, picnic tables, fire rings
Fee per night: $$$–$$$$
Pets: Permitted at some sites

Balanced Rock, a huge boulder perched on the edge of a cliff, is a famous landmark at Trough Creek State Park.

Activities: Hiking, fishing, hunting

Management: Pennsylvania Department of Conservation and Natural Resources

Contact: (814) 658-3847; www.dcnr.state.pa.us/stateparks/findapark/troughcreek/index.htm. For reservations call toll-free (888) 727-2757 or visit VisitPaParks.com.

Finding the campground: From Huntingdon travel 15.6 miles south on Route 26. Turn left/east onto Route 994 and go 5.2 miles. Turn left onto Little Valley Road and go 1.6 miles to the park.

GPS coordinates: N40 32.633' / W78 12.756'

Other: The park rents Trough Creek Lodge, a two-story stone home that was built in the 1800s as an ironmaster's mansion.

About the campground: The campground offers plenty of space between sites, making it a great place for a quiet weekend.

Why it's worth a visit: A number of geological wonders make this park worth exploring. There's the Ice Mine, a natural refrigerator that for years was a source of ice year-round. That's not so true now, but you can still step down into the mine and feel a dramatic change in temperature. There's also Balanced Rock, a huge boulder seemingly precariously perched on the edge of a cliff, and Copperas Rocks, a gorge where the cliff's rocks are covered with a coppery-yellow stain as a result of leaching sulfates. A number of hiking trails take you to these wonders.

Whenever you're out on the trails or elsewhere, be on the lookout for an oddity particular to this park: piebald deer. They are white-tailed deer that, rather than being brown with white bellies, are splotched with white all over. They can turn up anywhere, but this park seems to have more than its share.

80 Raystown Lake Susquehannock Campground

Location: South of Huntingdon
Season: Thurs before Memorial Day weekend to Labor Day; reservations required
Sites: 61, some ADA accessible and some tents only
Maximum RV length: 75 feet
Facilities: Vault toilets, water, picnic tables, fire rings
Fee per night: $$–$$$
Pets: Leashed pets permitted
Activities: Boating, swimming, hiking, biking, fishing, hunting
Management: US Army Corps of Engineers, Baltimore District
Contact: (814) 658-3405; www.nab.usace.army.mil/Raystown/. For reservations call toll-free (877) 444-6777 or visit www.recreation.gov.
Finding the campground: From Huntingdon head south on Route 26 for 7.5 miles. At Hesston turn left onto Seven Points Drive and travel 2.7 miles before turning left onto Bakers Hollow Road. Take the first right and follow the signs to the campground.
GPS coordinates: N40 39.716' / W78 03.812'
Other: Be sure to check out the visitor center—a two-story facility with wildlife mounts, interactive computer games, audiovisual presentations, a store, and more.
About the campground: A number of the sites here offer waterfront views and are within 10 to 30 feet of the lakeshore.
Why it's worth a visit: Located along the north-central part of the lake, near Mile Marker 7, this primitive campground is good if you want to get away from the large-scale, almost industrial mega-camps. That of course means fewer amenities, but you don't have to go completely primitive. For example, campers are allowed to use the hot showers at the Seven Points Beach changing house and the coin-operated laundry at the Seven Points Campground, just a 10-minute drive away.

The campground is also close to some of Raystown's hiking trails, including the 32-mile Alle-grippis Trail, which can be hiked in sections. And while you're here, check with the visitor center for a list of overlooks located throughout the area. Hawn's Overlook, just a 300-foot walk from the parking lot, is spectacular, especially at sunset.

81 Raystown Lake Seven Points Campground

Location: Southwest of Huntingdon
Season: First weekend of Apr through last weekend of Oct; reservations required
Sites: 261, some ADA accessible and some walk-in only
Maximum RV length: 75 feet

Facilities: Flush toilets, warm showers, water, electric hookups, sanitary dump station, picnic tables, fire rings, boat launch, boat rentals, playgrounds, visitor center, full service marina with restaurant

Fee per night: $$$$

Pets: Leashed pets permitted

Activities: Boating, swimming, waterskiing, tubing, hiking, biking, fishing, hunting, environmental education programs

Management: US Army Corps of Engineers, Baltimore District

Contact: (814) 658-3405; www.nab.usace.army.mil/Raystown/. For reservations call toll-free (877) 444-6777 or visit www.recreation.gov.

Finding the campground: From Huntingdon head south on Route 26 for 7.5 miles. At Hesston turn left onto Seven Points Drive and go about 4 miles to the campground.

GPS coordinates: N40 38.306'/W78 07.833'

Other: Bay loop is smallest, with some tent-only sites. Ridge loop is farthest from the water but closest to hiking trails. Point and Senoia loops are the most popular.

About the campground: This six-loop campground is Raystown's most modern and most popular. It's part of the larger Seven Points Recreation Area, the main hub of activity for the lake. The campground is always busy, which is why reservations are required.

Why it's worth a visit: At 28 miles long and 8,300 acres, Raystown Lake is the largest lake located completely in Pennsylvania. Fed by the Raystown Branch of the Juniata River, it offers excellent fishing for species such as muskies, smallmouth and largemouth bass, brown trout, and, most especially, striped bass. We're talking big fish: stripers up to thirty-plus pounds.

Water sports of all kinds, from waterskiing to tubing, are hugely popular too. And if you get away from the water, there's some wonderful hiking and mountain biking to be found on the Alle-grippis, Old Loggers, Hillside Nature, and Terrace Mountain Trails.

82 Raystown Lake Nancy's Campground

Location: South of Huntingdon

Season: Year-round; reservations required Apr through Oct

Sites: 50, all boat-in only

Maximum RV length: N/A

Facilities: Vault toilets, picnic table, fire rings

Fee per night: $–$$

Pets: Leashed pets permitted

Activities: Boating, hiking, fishing, hunting

Management: US Army Corps of Engineers, Baltimore District

Contact: (814) 658-3405; www.nab.usace.army.mil/Raystown/. No reservations accepted—it's first come, first served—but you can call the ranger station at (814) 658-6809 to check on availability.

Finding the campground: The campground is located at the lake's midpoint, between Mile Markers 15 and 16 in the western shore. Most boaters who come here launch from the James Creek launch for its proximity and parking. To get there follow Route 26 south from Huntingdon for 13.3

The largest impoundment of water totally within Pennsylvania, Raystown Lake draws corresponding crowds of boaters, as evidenced by the scene at Seven Points Marina.

miles. Turn left onto Fouses Crossing Road and go 0.9 mile. Turn left to stay on Fouses Crossing and go another 0.4 mile. Turn left onto James Creek Road and go 0.6 mile to the boat launch. **GPS coordinates:** N40 35.155'/W78 14.524'

Other: There are no showers here, but campers can use those at the Seven Points Beach changing house near Mile Marker 9.

About the campground: Sites are largely undefined and vary in size, but each site is marked in general by a post. The campground is nestled among mature trees opening up to a grassy shoreline.

Why it's worth a visit: Its relative solitude makes this campground special. That's not to say you'll be all alone here. A surprising number of people overnight on Raystown, both in the campground and simply by anchoring on the lake. That's why quiet hours are in effect lakewide from 10 p.m. to 6 a.m. But this area offers some peace, especially on weekdays.

Mooring areas are located on the north and south edges of the campground. To help you find your way, the local Friends of Raystown Lake group maintains nighttime navigational lights, marking major points and bends along the main channel. Green lights are located on the eastern (mountain) side of the lake; red lights are on the western side.

83 Shawnee State Park

Location: West of Bedford
Season: 8 months; second Fri in Apr through mid-Dec
Sites: 212, some ADA accessible and some walk-in only
Maximum RV length: 45 feet
Facilities: Flush toilets, warm showers, water, sanitary dump station, picnic tables, fire rings, washtubs, disc golf course, camp store
Fee per night: $$$–$$$$
Pets: Permitted at some sites
Activities: Swimming, boating, hiking, biking, fishing, hunting, environmental education programs
Management: Pennsylvania Department of Conservation and Natural Resources
Contact: (814) 733-4218; www.dcnr.state.pa.us/stateparks/findapark/shawnee/index.htm. For reservations call toll-free (888) 727-2757 or visit VisitPaParks.com.
Finding the campground: From Bedford head west on US 30 for about 7 miles; turn left onto State Park Road.

A kayaker makes his way around Shawnee Lake, the 451-acre centerpiece of Shawnee State Park.

GPS coordinates: N40 02.290' / W78 63.924'

Other: The park rents camping cottages, yurts, and a two-story house overlooking Shawnee Lake and has an organized group tenting area.

About the campground: This very large campground is divided into a series of loops. Sites are a mix of woods and open space, fairly close together. It now has full-service sites.

Why it's worth a visit: This park was named for the Native Americans who lived here for a while during their migration from the Potomac to the Ohio country in the 1700s. As with any park that has a lake as big as Shawnee's 451-acre impoundment, opportunities to fish and boat are the big draw. The lake is home to largemouth and smallmouth bass, northern pike, walleyes, catfish, and panfish. And there's some fine paddling here if you like to canoe or kayak. Only electric motors are permitted, so the water is calm and pleasant.

But don't overlook hiking in the park. Sixteen miles of trails wind through woods that are especially beautiful in fall. White-tailed deer and turkeys are commonly seen, as are all manner of songbirds. Check out the park's disc golf course too. The nine-hole course has some challenges, including one hole that involves going up and over a hill.

84 Cowans Gap State Park

Location: West of Chambersburg

Season: Second Fri in Apr through mid-Dec

Sites: 201, some walk-in only in area B and some ADA accessible in both A and B

Maximum RV length: 40 feet

Facilities: Flush toilets, warm showers, water, electric hookups, sanitary dump station, picnic tables, fire rings, courtesy boat mooring area for registered campers

Fee per night: $$$–$$$$

Pets: Permitted at some sites

Activities: Boating, swimming, hiking, fishing, hunting, environmental education programs

Management: Pennsylvania Department of Conservation and Natural Resources

Contact: (717) 485-3948; www.dcnr.state.pa.us/stateparks/findapark/cowansgap/index.htm. For reservations call toll-free (888) 727-2757 or visit VisitPaParks.com.

Finding the campground: From Chambersburg follow US 30 west for 13.8 miles. Turn right onto Path Valley Road/Route 75 and go 6.1 miles. Turn left onto Stumpy Lane and go 1.5 miles. Continue for another 0.1 mile after Stumpy Lane becomes Aughwick Road/Route 1005.

GPS coordinates: N39 99.544' / W77 92.491'

Other: The park has 10 rustic cabins for rent and an organized group tenting area.

About the campground: Camping area A is larger and more about maximizing space. Camping area B is smaller and closer to the lake; the walk-in sites are located here.

Why it's worth a visit: Cowans Gap is interesting geologically in terms of how it was formed. Most gaps—a notch or pass between two mountains—are water gaps, with a river or stream flowing through them. Cowans Gap is a wind gap. It had a stream once, millions of years ago. But after it created the gap, the landscape shifted, leaving Cowans Gap dry.

Today visitors to the park can experience it in one of two ways. Want to swim, fish, or boat in the 42-acre lake; picnic; or engage in one of the park's environmental programs? You can do all those things in the day-use areas, which get the most traffic. Want more solitude? You can hike some of the park's 11 miles of trails. Several run around the park's edges and are relatively rugged. Geyer Trail is surprisingly tough for being only 0.5 mile long, but it's beautiful in June when the mountain laurel's in bloom. Plessinger Trail, 1.1 miles long, is another rough one, but it parallels Aughwick Creek, a very nice trout stream. And 1.3-mile Knobsville Road Trail leads to an overlook and interpretive exhibit.

85 Caledonia State Park

Location: East of Chambersburg
Season: Opens first Fri after Mar 28 and runs through the last Sun in Oct for the Chinquapin Campground and through deer season (usually mid-Dec) for the Hosack Run Campground
Sites: 175, some ADA accessible, in two sites: Chinquapin and Hosack Run Campgrounds
Maximum RV length: 60 feet
Facilities: Flush toilets, warm showers, water, electric hookups, sanitary dump station, picnic tables, fire rings, 18-hole golf course, large ADA accessible pool with a water slide and snack bar
Fee per night: $$$–$$$$
Pets: Permitted in Hosack Run but not in Chinquapin
Activities: Swimming, hiking, fishing, hunting, environmental education programs
Management: Pennsylvania Department of Conservation and Natural Resources
Contact: (717) 352-2161; www.dcnr.state.pa.us/stateparks/findapark/caledonia/index.htm. For reservations call toll-free (888) 727-2757 or visit VisitPaParks.com.
Finding the campground: From Chambersburg follow US 30 east for 10.1 miles. Turn left onto Pine Grove Road/Route 233 and go 0.2 mile. Take the first left into the park.
GPS coordinates: N39 90.894'/W77 47.799' for Chinquapin; N39 91.464'/W77 46.829' for Hosack Run
Other: The park offers one two-story home for rent and has an organized group tenting area.
About the campground: Chinquapin Campground is on a wooded hillside, shaded and close to the pool. Hosack Run Campground is moderately level and 1 mile from the day-use area. Both campgrounds were recently renovated to include new shower and restroom facilities, new dump stations, and full hookup sites with water, sewer, and electric.
Why it's worth a visit: This park has some interesting history. Located just west of Gettysburg, it was the site of an iron furnace, forge, mill, and other industry, all established by famous abolitionist Thaddeus Stevens. When Confederate troops passed through the area just prior to the battle of Gettysburg in 1863, cavalry officer Jubal Early ordered that it all be burned to the ground on the premise that it was of aid to the enemy. Later the state bought the land and leased it to a group that made it a trolley stop with amusement rides and a dance pavilion.

Today the park remains unique for one particular reason: It's home to the only eighteen-hole golf course located within a Pennsylvania state park. Built in the 1920s, the par-68 course is one of the oldest in south-central Pennsylvania. The Pennsylvania Forest Fire Museum Association has a small museum across from the park office now, with plans in the works to build a much larger discovery center.

86 Pine Grove Furnace State Park

Location: Southwest of Mount Holly Springs
Season: Last weekend in Mar to mid-Dec
Sites: 70, some ADA accessible
Maximum RV length: 60 feet; however, most sites and campground roads cannot accommodate RVs over 30 feet. Consult individual site attributes when making reservations.
Facilities: Flush toilets, warm showers, water hydrants, electricity, sanitary dump station, picnic tables, fire rings, boat concession, 2 beaches, seasonal camp store, Appalachian Trail Museum, Ironmaster's Mansion (serves as a hostel), Paymaster's Cabin
Fee per night: $$$-$$$$
Pets: Permitted at some sites
Activities: Boating, swimming, hiking, biking, fishing, hunting, environmental education programs
Management: Pennsylvania Department of Conservation and Natural Resources
Contact: (717) 486-7174; www.dcnr.state.pa.us/stateparks/findapark/pinegrovefurnace/index .htm. For reservations call toll-free (888) 727-2757 or visit VisitPaParks.com.

Paddlers are all smiles as they make their way around Laurel Lake, the larger of Pine Grove Furnace State Park's two lakes.

Finding the campground: From Mount Holly Springs go south on Route 34 for 2.6 miles. Turn right onto Pine Grove Road and go 6.7 miles to the park.

GPS coordinates: N40 02.479' / W77 31.122'

Other: This park offers the Paymaster's Cabin, a modern facility, for rent and has a hostel in the old Ironmaster's Mansion. There's an organized group tenting area too. The Appalachian Trail (AT) passes through the park.

About the campground: Charcoal Hearth Campground, as the facility here is known, has pet-specific sites for both tents and RVs. Some have electric, some do not.

Why it's worth a visit: Site of yet another old ironworks that was turned into a park by the Civilian Conservation Corps, this park is home to the Appalachian Trail Museum. The AT stretches 2,184 miles from Georgia to Maine. The museum sits at about the trail's midpoint. It offers exhibits, a variety of public programs, and a hands-on area for children. You can learn more about the museum before you go by visiting www.atmuseum.org.

There are several shorter trails within the park also worth exploring, as well as some interesting fishing and boating. Pine Grove Furnace has two lakes. The larger, 25-acre Laurel Lake, is good for fishing and paddling. A boat concession there caters to those without their own boats. Fuller Lake allows shoreline fishing but no boating.

87 Fowlers Hollow State Park

Location: North of Shippensburg

Season: 8 months; mid-Apr to mid-Dec

Sites: 17, some ADA accessible and some walk-in only

Maximum RV length: 50 feet

Facilities: Flush toilets, water, sanitary dump station, picnic tables, fire rings

Fee per night: $$$–$$$$

Pets: Permitted at some sites

Activities: Hiking, mountain biking, horseback riding, fishing, hunting

Management: Pennsylvania Department of Conservation and Natural Resources

Contact: (717) 776-5272; www.dcnr.state.pa.us/stateparks/findapark/fowlershollow/index.htm. For reservations call toll-free (888) 727-2757 or visit VisitPaParks.com.

Finding the campground: From Shippensburg follow Route 696 for 2 miles. Turn left onto Middle Spring Road and go 0.7 mile. Turn left onto McClays Mill Road; go 1.9 miles and turn right onto Paxton Run Road. Go 2.7 miles; turn left onto Newburg Road/Route 641 and go 10.2 miles before turning left onto Spring Run Road/Route 641 and continuing for 1.6 miles. Turn right onto Path Valley Road/Route 75 and go 7 miles. Turn right onto Big Spring Road/Route 274 and go 9 miles. Turn right onto Upper Buck Ridge Road; go 2.1 miles and turn right onto Fowlers Hollow Run Road.

GPS coordinates: N40 27.637' / W77 57.925'

Other: This park was the site of large-scale logging a century ago. A portable sawmill was used to cut trees, including hemlocks, even the bark of which was used in various products.

About the campground: This small campground has its sites in a row. The walk-in tent sites are all wooded.

Why it's worth a visit: This small narrow park—it's a rectangular 104 acres—provides opportunities to fish Fowlers Hollow Run for brook trout early in spring or to camp here and ride your horse or bike or hike. There's also a large playfield in the day-use area, where you'll find grills for cooking.

This park serves primarily as a launch point for exploring the adjacent Tuscarora State Forest. It's very popular with hunters, who come here looking for deer and turkeys. The Anderson Ridge Limited Access Buck Hunting Area is a draw for those looking for a wilderness hunt; it's a 6,000-acre chunk of forest where all motorized vehicles are prohibited.

There's some fine hiking here as well. One of the more interesting paths is also one of the shortest. At just 1 mile, Tunnel Trail leads to the ruins of two narrow-gauge railroads.

88 Colonel Denning State Park

Location: North of Newville
Season: Mid-Apr to mid-Dec
Sites: 49, some walk-in only
Maximum RV length: 40 feet
Facilities: Vault toilets, water, sanitary dump station, picnic tables, fire rings. Firewood and ice for sale from the campground host
Fee per night: $$$-$$$$
Pets: Permitted at some sites
Activities: Boating, swimming, hiking, orienteering, fishing, hunting
Management: Pennsylvania Department of Conservation and Natural Resources
Contact: (717) 776-5272; www.dcnr.state.pa.us/stateparks/findapark/coloneldenning/index .htm. For reservations call toll-free (888) 727-2757 or visit VisitPaParks.com.
Finding the campground: From Newville follow Route 233 north for 8.8 miles to the park.
GPS coordinates: N40 28.140'/W77 41.559'
Other: The park is located in Doubling Gap, so named because Blue Mountain doubles back on itself in an S-turn.
About the campground: This is a generally roomy campsite, with only the tent sites being fairly close together. There's also an organized group tenting area.
Why it's worth a visit: This is another great park for hiking, with 18 miles of trails. The 2.5-mile Flat Rock Trail rises to a scenic vista of the Cumberland Valley. Another trail leads to an overlook where you can see the "S" in the Doubling Gap. A hiking and nature trail guide, available at the park office, explains where these and other trails go and what you can expect to see along the way of each one.

If you want to test your ability to go off the beaten path, you can do that too. The park has three orienteering courses, one each for those with beginning, intermediate, and advanced skills. Course outlines are available at the office.

The park also hosts a summer concert series. It's a fun time. Local bands play on the park lawn for audiences who set up chairs or spread blankets on the ground and eat and drink goods from a concession stand. The concerts are free, although the park's Friends group accepts donations, with the proceeds used to pay for improvements to park facilities.

89 Little Buffalo State Park

Location: North of Carlisle
Season: Mid-Apr through third Sun in Oct
Sites: 45, some ADA accessible
Maximum RV length: 55 feet
Facilities: Flush toilets, warm showers, water, electricity, sanitary dump station, picnic tables, fire rings, swimming pool
Fee per night: $$$–$$$$
Pets: Permitted at all sites
Activities: Boating, hiking, Volksmarching, fishing, hunting, environmental education programs, Old Fashioned Apple Festival, Halloween Night, Christmas Walk
Management: Pennsylvania Department of Conservation and Natural Resources
Contact: (717) 567-9255; www.dcnr.state.pa.us/stateparks/findapark/littlebuffalo/index.htm. For reservations call toll-free (888) 727-2757 or visit VisitPaParks.com.
Finding the campground: From Carlisle go north on Route 34 for 19.7 miles. Turn right onto East Main Street/Route 34 and go another 1.8 miles. Turn left onto State Park Road and go 1.5 miles to the campground.
GPS coordinates: N40 45.674'/W77 18.934'
Other: The park has camping cottages and one modern cabin for rent.
About the campground: A little pond within walking distance of the campground is a neat place to look for frogs and other wildlife. Two sites offer full hookups, three are walk-in.
Why it's worth a visit: This park—which has a butterfly garden that's worth a look and a huge swimming pool that can handle almost 1,300 people—is also home to an official Volksmarching trail, created by an affiliate of the American Volksport Association. The group blazes 6.2- and 3.1-mile trails and then holds noncompetitive walks along them. It serves to bring walkers together for companionship while they're out and about in the woods and fields. The trail here is a loop made up of a number of trails within the park.

While you're here, be sure to look for some of the park's colorful wildlife too. Ospreys are regular visitors, if not residents, and wood ducks nest in hollow trees on the lake's edge. Perhaps the most unusual critter—one often caught by children in the streams around the park, especially the channel below the dam—is the red-spotted newt, or red eft. These amphibians can reach 5 inches in length. What's neat is that as juveniles they are bright orange with outlined red spots. As adults they turn olive green and their tails flatten, but they still retain their telltale spots. You'll often see them basking as they float on the surface of the water. They're not hard to catch, but if you handle one, be sure to wash your hands afterward to wash away the mild toxin they emit as defense against hungry predators.

90 Penn-Roosevelt State Park

Location: South of Potters Mills
Season: Mid-Apr to mid-Nov
Sites: 18, for tents only; some walk-in only

Maximum RV length: N/A
Facilities: Vault toilets, water, picnic tables, fire rings
Fee per night: $$-$$$$
Pets: Permitted at some sites
Activities: Hiking, horseback riding, fishing, hunting
Management: Pennsylvania Department of Conservation and Natural Resources
Contact: (814) 667-1800; www.dcnr.state.pa.us/stateparks/findapark/pennroosevelt/index.htm. No reservations accepted; it's first come, first served.
Finding the campground: From Potters Mills turn south off US 322 onto Crowfield Road. Go 6 miles to the park.
GPS coordinates: N40 72.659'/W77 70.055'
Other: The 3.5-acre pond holds some native brook trout. They're not big, but they are fun to catch.
About the campground: Sites 11 and 12 offer the most privacy. Registration is done on the honor system.
Why it's worth a visit: This 41-acre park is located in an isolated area of the Seven Mountains region known as the Stone Creek Kettle. But it's surrounded by 97,000-acre Rothrock State Forest, so if you're looking for low-impact, quiet, isolated recreation, this is a wonderful place to visit. The Rothrock is home to seven state-designated natural areas and one wild area. Visit them to see old-growth white pine and hemlock stands, talus, limestone and sandstone slopes, and mountain laurel. Just be aware that the roads to this park are not plowed in winter, so access can be iffy in bad weather.

Check out the Civilian Conservation Corps monument. Several parks around the state have similar memorials. What makes the camp memorialized here unique is that during segregation in the 1930s, it was one of just twelve African American camps in the state.

91 Greenwood Furnace State Park

Location: South of State College
Season: Second Fri in Apr through end of Oct
Sites: 48, some ADA accessible and some walk-in only
Maximum RV length: 40 feet
Facilities: Flush toilets, warm showers, water, electricity, sanitary dump station, picnic tables, fire rings, dishwashing sinks in the shower house, amphitheater, blacksmith shop, visitor center and gift shop
Fee per night: $$$-$$$$
Pets: Permitted at some sites
Activities: Boating, swimming, hiking, orienteering, environmental education programs, historic walking tour, fishing, hunting
Management: Pennsylvania Department of Conservation and Natural Resources
Contact: (814) 667-1800; www.dcnr.state.pa.us/stateparks/findapark/greenwoodfurnace/index .htm. For reservations call toll-free (888) 727-2757 or visit VisitPaParks.com.
Finding the campground: From State College head south on Route 26 for 5.4 miles. Turn left onto Water Street/Route 26; go 2 miles and continue 7.4 miles after Route 26 becomes McAlevy's Fort Road. Turn left onto Greenwood Road/Route 305 and go 4.9 miles.

Furnace stack #2 at Greenwood Furnace State Park last burned in 1904, but visitors can still see it and other remnants of the old ironmaking village.

GPS coordinates: N40 64.634' / W77 76.042'

Other: This park has a gift shop if you want to take something home.

About the campground: The walk-in sites offer the most privacy.

Why it's worth a visit: What do you get when you combine a park with a lake, trails, and woods with the remains of an industrial town? Greenwood Furnace State Park. It takes its name from an ironworks that existed here for seventy years in the nineteenth century. At one time there were 127 buildings in the village. Several remain, including the ironmaster's house, some of the furnaces and charcoal facilities, and a schoolhouse. You can explore on your own, take part in one of the historic walking tours offered, or visit the free Old Home Days Heritage Festival held the first weekend in August. Then you'll find historical interpreters, demonstrations, musical programs, and lots of good food.

The park also offers some nice hiking on a variety of trails. There are 25 miles altogether, some hiking only and some open to skiing and snowmobiling in winter.

92 Reeds Gap State Park

Location: East of Milroy
Season: Second Fri in Apr to third Sun in Oct
Sites: 14
Maximum RV length: N/A
Facilities: Vault toilets, showers nearby, water
Fee per night: $$$-$$$$
Pets: Permitted at all sites
Activities: Hiking, fishing, hunting, environmental education programs
Management: Pennsylvania Department of Conservation and Natural Resources
Contact: (717) 677-3622; www.dcnr.state.pa.us/stateparks/findapark/reedsgap/index.htm. For reservations call toll-free (888) 727-2757 or visit VisitPaParks.com.
Finding the campground: From US 322 in Milroy, exit onto New Lancaster Valley Road and go 7 miles to the park.
GPS coordinates: N40 72.119'/W77 47.080'
Other: This parks hosts a "Kid's Day" festival each year in mid-October, right before the campground closes.
About the campground: The campground accommodates tents only.
Why it's worth a visit: This park, surrounded by Bald Eagle State Forest, is quaint, quiet, and relaxing. Honey Creek splits it from end to end and offers decent fishing for stocked trout, especially in spring, and is paralleled by hiking trails on both sides. Bridges cross the stream at four points, so you can hike upstream, fish the length of the stream, and then cross over and walk back or shorten the trip at various points. And try casting your line into some of the smaller tributary streams that flow into Honey Creek. Many hold populations of wild trout.

If you're hiking, be sure to check out the ruins of the old water storage dam that dates to the mid-1800s, when a water-powered sawmill operated here at the southwest end of the park.

93 Poe Valley State Park

Location: South of Millheim
Season: Second Fri in Apr to mid-Dec
Sites: 45, some ADA accessible
Maximum RV length: 40 feet
Facilities: Flush toilets, warm showers, water, electricity, sanitary dump station, picnic tables, fire rings
Fee per night: $$$-$$$$
Pets: Permitted at some sites
Activities: Boating, swimming, hiking, fishing, hunting, environmental education programs
Management: Pennsylvania Department of Conservation and Natural Resources
Contact: (814) 349-2460; www.dcnr.state.pa.us/stateparks/findapark/poevalley/index.htm. For reservations call toll-free (888) 727-2757 or visit VisitPaParks.com.

Finding the campground: From Millheim go west on East Main Street/Route 45 for 1.6 miles. Turn left onto Paradise Road (the roads are unpaved from here on) and go 2.2 miles. Continue 0.6 mile as Paradise becomes Greenbriar Gap Road and then 1.8 miles as Greenbriar becomes Siglerville Millheim Pike. Turn left onto Pine Swamp Road and go 3.9 miles. Make a slight right onto Poe Valley Road. Go less than a mile; the entrance to the park and the campground will be on your right.

GPS coordinates: N40 82.216'/W77 46.786'

Other: The park rents camping cottages and a deluxe camping cottage.

About the campground: This is a loop campground located adjacent to the dam and spillway at Poe Lake. All sites are withing walking distance of all other park facilities.

Why it's worth a visit: Surrounded by 198,000-acre Bald Eagle State Forest, this is a small, 620-acre patch of woods surrounded by a whole lot more woods. You can find solitude here or use this as a base camp for a larger adventure. Nearby is the famous Penns Creek, Pennsylvania's longest limestone trout stream and one revered by fly-fishermen for its famous eastern green drake hatch. It holds wild brown trout and stocked fish too. There's some decent stocked trout fishing to be had in 25-acre Poe Lake in spring as well.

Poe Lake is also fun to paddle around in a canoe or kayak, especially early in the morning and right at dusk, when wildlife tends to be more active and a quiet approach is often the ticket to some up-close encounters.

94 Poe Paddy State Park

Location: South of Millheim

Season: Second Fri in Apr to mid-Dec

Sites: 36

Maximum RV length: 40 feet

Facilities: Vault toilets, water, picnic tables, fire rings, sanitary dump station available at nearby Poe Valley State Park. For a fee, campers can shower at Poe Valley, too.

Fee per night: $$$-$$$$

Pets: Permitted at some sites

Activities: Hiking, fishing

Management: Pennsylvania Department of Conservation and Natural Resources

Contact: (717) 667-3622; www.dcnr.state.pa.us/stateparks/findapark/poepaddy/index.htm. For reservations call toll-free (888) 727-2757 or visit VisitPaParks.com.

Finding the campground: Go west on East Main Street/Route 45 for 1.6 miles. Turn left onto Paradise Road and go 2.2 miles. Continue onto Greenbriar Gap Road for another 0.6 mile (portions of the road from here on out are unpaved) to where Greenbriar becomes Siglerville Millheim Pike. Go 1.8 miles; turn left onto Pine Swamp Road and go 3.9 miles. Make a sharp left onto Poe Valley Road; go 2.4 miles and turn left onto Poe Valley Drive. The campground will be on your left in less than a mile.

GPS coordinates: N40 83.516'/W77 41.851'

Other: This park gets its unusual name from Poe Mountain to the west and Paddy Mountain to the east.

About the campground: There are no paved roads leading to the park, so access in winter and on its edges can be iffy. The sanitary dump station for this park is located in nearby Poe Valley State Park. There's an organized group tenting area here, along with two Adirondack-style shelters.

Why it's worth a visit: As is the case at Poe Valley, the biggest draw here is the trout fishing on Penns Creek. This classic riffle and pool water is probably the best, and best-loved, trout stream in a state where trout are more popular among anglers than any other species. Late May or early June—when the legendary green drake hatch comes off—is the best time to be on the water.

Hikers looking for the unusual or special will find something for themselves as well. The Mid State Trail passes through here, going through the 250-foot-long Paddy Mountain Railroad Tunnel along the way.

95 Raymond B. Winter State Park

Location: West of Lewisburg
Season: Second Fri in Apr through mid-Dec
Sites: 61, some ADA accessible and some walk-in only
Maximum RV length: 40 feet
Facilities: Flush toilets, warm showers, water, electricity, sanitary dump station, picnic tables, fire rings, lantern holder, playground
Fee per night: $$$–$$$$
Pets: Permitted at some sites
Activities: Swimming, hiking, mountain biking, fishing, hunting, environmental education programs
Management: Pennsylvania Department of Conservation and Natural Resources
Contact: (570) 966-1455; www.dcnr.state.pa.us/stateparks/findapark/raymondbwinter/index .htm. For reservations call toll-free (888) 727-2757 or visit VisitPaParks.com.
Finding the campground: From Lewisburg head west on Route 192 for 17.6 miles. Pass the park office and Halfway Lake and make a left onto Boyer Gap Road and then an immediate left onto Keystone Road. Go less than 1 mile and the campground entrance will be on the right.
GPS coordinates: N40 99.234' / W77 18.758'
Other: The park rents camping cottages.
About the campground: The sites closest to the camping cottages offer the most space. There are two walk-in sites near the Old Boundary Trail.
Why it's worth a visit: Be sure to explore the Rapid Run Natural Area. One of the first places in the state set aside to be maintained in an undisturbed condition, it's 39 acres are home to white pines and hemlocks indicative of Pennsylvania's forests of the 1850s. Here you'll also find vernal ponds—temporary pools of water in the woods that dry up in summer. Before that happens the pools support fairy shrimp, wood frogs, spotted salamanders, and assorted insects. A discovery guide available at the park office or learning center describes the area's 1-mile trail and offers suggestions on how best to explore it.

A couple other unusual geologic features worth exploring are the Little Bubbler and Park Overlook. The former is a small boiling spring visible at the west end of the swimming beach. It's an artesian spring that causes sand to bubble and churn in the rising water. The overlook offers views of Halfway Dam, the Rapid Run water gap, and several nearby mountains. Reach it by hiking Overlook Trail or driving McCalls Dam Road.

A great blue heron is reflected in the waters of Pinchot Lake at Gifford Pinchot State Park.

96 Gifford Pinchot State Park

Location: South of Harrisburg
Season: Second Fri in Apr to end of Oct
Sites: 284, some ADA accessible
Maximum RV length: 65 feet
Facilities: Flush toilets, warm showers, water, electricity, sanitary dump station, picnic tables, fire rings, 2 disc golf courses
Fee per night: $$$-$$$$
Pets: Permitted at some sites
Activities: Boating, swimming, hiking, biking, horseback riding, disc golf, fishing, hunting, environmental education programs
Management: Pennsylvania Department of Conservation and Natural Resources
Contact: (717) 432-5011; www.dcnr.state.pa.us/stateparks/findapark/giffordpinchot/index.htm. For reservations call toll-free (888) 727-2757 or visit VisitPaParks.com.
Finding the campground: From Harrisburg follow I-83 south for 8.1 miles. Take exit 35 toward Route 177/Lewisbury, go 0.1 mile. Turn right onto Yorktown Road and go 0.1 mile. Take the first left onto Wyndamere Road/Route 177. Follow Route 177 for 6.8 miles to the park.
GPS coordinates: N40 05.803'/W76 90.181'
Other: The park rents camping cottages, yurts, and 10 modern cabins and has an organized group tenting site.
About the campground: This is one of the largest public campgrounds in the state. You won't find a lot of privacy, but there are numerous lakeside sites.
Why it's worth a visit: This more than 2,300-acre expanse is billed as a "full-service" park in that if there's anything you can think of to do on a camping trip, you can probably do it here. There's boating, hiking, hunting, fishing, and more. What's more, you can pick your activity and often get some guidance in doing it. The park hosts numerous environmental education programs throughout the camping season, including everything from kayaking classes to pontoon boat tours to the annual Halloween "Pinchoteen" festival, which offers games, pumpkin carving, a scavenger hunt, and more. The park is also home to two eighteen-hole disc golf courses.

There's some unique wildlife here too. Giant swallowtail butterflies, the largest butterfly found in North America, are frequent visitors here during the warmer months. Hiking some of the park's 18 miles of trails will often give you a glimpse of these creatures. Roughly 1,800 acres of parkland are open to hunting, but only bows are legal until November 1, at which time shotguns and muzzleloaders are also allowed.

97 Codorus State Park

Location: East of Hanover
Season: Second Fri in Apr to Nov 1
Sites: 193, some ADA accessible and some walk-in only
Maximum RV length: 54 feet

Facilities: Flush toilets, warm showers, water, electricity, sanitary dump station, picnic tables, fire rings, boat rental, swimming pool, disc golf course

Fee per night: $$$-$$$$

Pets: Permitted at some sites

Activities: Boating, scuba diving, hiking, mountain biking, horseback riding, fishing, hunting, disc golf, environmental education programs

Management: Pennsylvania Department of Conservation and Natural Resources

Contact: (717) 637-2816; www.dcnr.state.pa.us/stateparks/findapark/codorus/index.htm. For reservations call toll-free (888) 727-2757 or visit VisitPaParks.com.

Finding the campground: From Hanover follow Route 116/York Street east for 1.5 miles. Turn right onto Blooming Grove Road/Route 216 and go a little more than 3 miles. Just past Swimming Pool Road, turn right onto Dubs Church Road, staying right at the next T, and the campground entrance will be on the right.

GPS coordinates: N39 77.500'/W76 91.348'

Other: The park rents camping cottages and yurts.

About the campground: This campground is a series of loops, with a "tail" set aside for tent campers. A boat launch for use exclusively by registered campers is available.

Why it's worth a visit: This is a big park with a big lake—the 1,275-acre Lake Marburg. Much of what goes on in the park centers around that water, which interestingly is owned by a local paper company that still uses the impoundment for its water supply. You can boat in your own craft—the campground has its own boat launch—or a rented one and scuba dive in one cove or fish for such species as muskies and tiger muskies, largemouth bass, northern pike, and panfish. The lake and its surrounding wetlands are also a major draw for several bird species, including bald eagles, ospreys, and in fall large numbers of ruddy ducks, mergansers, and scaups.

The park is also home to a special disc golf course. Rated one of the most challenging courses in Pennsylvania, it has hosted the state championship several times. The course features fifty-four holes with paved tees and winds through fields and forests. There's even a mini disc golf course nearby for children.

98 Lancaster County Central Park

Location: Lancaster County Central Park, just south of Lancaster City

Season: Apr 1 to Oct 31

Sites: 5, for tents only

Maximum RV length: N/A

Facilities: Vault toilets, water, picnic tables, fire rings, grills, ball fields, fitness trail, tennis courts, skate park, garden plots, environmental center and library, archaeological site

Fee per night: $$$-$$$$

Pets: Permitted at all sites but must be kept on-leash

Activities: Boating, wading, hiking, biking, fishing, environmental education programs

Management: Lancaster County Department of Parks and Recreation

Contact: https://co.lancaster.pa.us/244/Lancaster-County-Central-Park. For reservations call (717) 299-8215.

Blooming tiger lilies provide a burst of color at Lancaster County Central Park.

Finding the campground: From Lancaster take Duke Street south through the city. Turn right onto Eshelman Mill Road. Stay right at the fork to remain on Eshelman. Turn right onto Nature's Way.
GPS coordinates: N40 01.305' / W76 27.842'
Other: At 544 acres this is Lancaster County's largest park, but the camping area takes in just 10 acres. An extra $10 gets you a 10- to 12-piece pile of firewood.
About the campground: Each site can accommodate up to eight people each. There is an additional charge per person for campers five through eight.
Why it's worth a visit: There are a number of hiking trails—including a fitness trail with exercise stations—and almost all of them offer easy to moderate walking. A guide available from the park describes what you might encounter along each trail.

The Conestoga River loops around the park and offers some good fishing and a nice, relaxing Class I float if you want to canoe or kayak. Mill Creek can also be fished. And if you just want to relax, the Shuts Environmental Library, housed in an eighteenth-century farmhouse, has 4,500-plus books and videos on nature, wildlife, gardening, Native Americans, health, wilderness survival, and other topics, as well as field guides, available to borrow.

99 French Creek State Park

Location: Southwest of Pottstown
Season: Mar 1 to Jan 2
Sites: 199, some ADA accessible
Maximum RV length: 50 feet
Facilities: Flush toilets, warm showers, water, electricity, sanitary dump station, picnic tables, fire rings, disc golf course
Fee per night: $$$-$$$$
Pets: Permitted at some sites
Activities: Boating, swimming, hiking, mountain biking, horseback riding, orienteering, disc golf, fishing, hunting, environmental education programs
Management: Pennsylvania Department of Conservation and Natural Resources
Contact: (610) 582-9680; www.dcnr.state.pa.us/stateparks/findapark/frenchcreek/index.htm. For reservations call toll-free (888) 727-2757 or visit VisitPaParks.com.

Framed by a bridge and dam, an angler fishes for trout on an April weekend in French Creek State Park.

Finding the campground: From Pottstown follow West Schuylkill Road/Route 724 west for 6.6 miles. Take a slight left onto Shed Road and go 0.5 mile; take the first left to stay on Shed Road. Go 2.5 miles; turn left onto Shed Road/Route 345/Hopewell Road and go 0.2 mile. Turn right onto Park Road and go 0.8 mile to the campground.

GPS coordinates: N40 21.100'/W75 78.335'

Other: The park rents camping cottages, yurts, and 10 modern cabins. It also has an organized group tenting area and organized group cabin camps.

About the campground: The campground here is wooded. All sites are relatively close together but still nice.

Why it's worth a visit: This park is an oasis of sorts—the only state park close to Philadelphia that offers camping. At more than 7,700 acres, it's also the largest contiguous block of forest between New York City and Washington, DC. That means it gets some heavy usage. But it's a nice place to visit and stay, with two lakes to fish and some cool hiking trails.

The 68-acre Hopewell Lake is home to warmwater species like bass, panfish, and pickerel; 22-acre Scotts Run Lake is a coldwater fishery stocked with trout. There are 35 miles of trails. The 6-mile Boone Trail presents some challenging walking, but it's worth it. The trail connects all the major attractions here, so if you're looking for one way to see what French Creek has to offer, this is the avenue. You can start it from the campground too, so that's convenient.

About 6,000 acres of the park are open to hunting, which also draws people, given the otherwise congested nature of this part of the state. Deer, turkeys, and small game are common species.

While in the area be sure to visit nearby Hopewell Furnace National Historic Site, an 1830s cold blast furnace. It's open year-round; historical interpreters work the site in summer to explain its history.

Appendix: Packing List

Who hasn't been there? You leave home, drive a considerable distance to your camp-site, and then realize you've left some essential piece of equipment at home. It might be your raincoat or your camp ax or a lighter for the stove and lanterns. Whatever it is, it's something you need and can't get readily.

To avoid that kind of frustration, print a copy of the following checklist and keep it in your camping bin or tote. You might want more than is listed here or less, depending on how you travel. But whenever you are planning to leave home, pull out the list and check off items as you pack them in your vehicle. That won't necessarily guarantee you'll always have everything you need on hand, but it will help.

Your list should include:

❏ Reservation paperwork. If you called ahead or reserved space online, take your receipt or confirmation with you.

❏ Backpack, day pack, and/or fanny pack

❏ Bags (reusable grocery bags, always handy for holding odds and ends)

❏ Ice chest with ice

❏ Lantern (with propane, liquid fuel, or batteries, as appropriate, and some extra mantles)

❏ Flashlights or headlamps, with batteries and spare bulbs

❏ Matches, preferably waterproof, and/or a lighter

❏ Tent

❏ Tent rain tarp

❏ Extra tent stakes

❏ Dining fly

❏ Plastic ground cloth for under the tent

❏ Sleeping bag

❏ Sleeping mattress or pad (along with a method of inflating it)

❏ Pillow

❏ Space blanket

❏ Sunscreen

❏ Insect repellent

❏ Poison ivy block

❏ Poison ivy remedies

❏ Allergy medicines

❏ Pain-relief pills, such as aspirin or acetaminophen

❏ Stomach medicines (for diarrhea, upset stomach, etc.)

- ❏ Tweezers for splinters
- ❏ Antiseptic
- ❏ Band-Aids and bandages
- ❏ Itch cream for bug bites
- ❏ Moleskin to prevent blisters if you hike a lot
- ❏ A first-aid kit that you can carry with you on a hike or canoe trip
- ❏ Prescription medicines
- ❏ Extra glasses or contact lenses and a glasses repair kit
- ❏ Washcloth
- ❏ Bath towel
- ❏ Biodegradable soap
- ❏ Biodegradable shampoo
- ❏ Biodegradable toothpaste
- ❏ Toothbrush
- ❏ Comb or hairbrush
- ❏ Razor and shaving cream
- ❏ Toilet paper (the stuff in state park campgrounds is notoriously cheap, earning more complaints from visitors than just about anything else)
- ❏ A case or bag for carrying everything to the shower house
- ❏ Bathing suit
- ❏ Water shoes
- ❏ Extra dry shoes
- ❏ Sunglasses
- ❏ Ax
- ❏ Bow saw
- ❏ Extension cord for campsites with an electrical hookup
- ❏ Duct tape and/or electrical tape
- ❏ Hammer for pounding in tent pegs
- ❏ Rope
- ❏ Clothesline and clothespins
- ❏ Whisk broom to clean table and tent site
- ❏ Pocketknife
- ❏ Compass and area map
- ❏ Fishing pole, gear, license, and lures or bait
- ❏ Beach chairs
- ❏ Camping chairs

- ❏ Safety pins
- ❏ Cell phone with your car adapter
- ❏ Camera with good batteries
- ❏ Camcorder, also with good batteries
- ❏ Money, credit card, and ID (to get your senior discount, if nothing else)
- ❏ Books, radio, cards, games, toys, etc.
- ❏ Sports equipment
- ❏ Citronella candles
- ❏ Binoculars
- ❏ Field guides for identifying wildlife
- ❏ Clothing appropriate for the season (Remember that it never hurts to have extra dry socks and an extra sweatshirt or jacket in case the nights get cooler than expected.)
- ❏ Wide-brimmed hat to block the sun
- ❏ Jacket
- ❏ Rain gear or poncho (which can double as an emergency lean-to if you're on the trail)
- ❏ Shower shoes
- ❏ Hiking boots
- ❏ Hiking staff
- ❏ Work gloves
- ❏ A few simple tools (hammer, pliers, tape, screwdrivers)
- ❏ Stove with fuel and lighter or charcoal and lighter fluid and grill
- ❏ Newspapers or some other tinder for lighting a campfire
- ❏ Firewood
- ❏ Frying pan with lid
- ❏ Cooking skewers for hot dogs, marshmallows, etc.
- ❏ Pot or saucepan with lid
- ❏ Can opener
- ❏ Tongs
- ❏ Coffeemaker and filters
- ❏ Pot lifter and/or potholders
- ❏ Tablecloth
- ❏ Plates
- ❏ Mugs/cups
- ❏ Knives, forks, spoons
- ❏ Kitchen knife

- ❏ Mixing bowl
- ❏ Spatula
- ❏ Scrub pad
- ❏ Dishpan for washing dishes
- ❏ Container for water
- ❏ Paper towels and napkins
- ❏ Trash bags
- ❏ Plastic bags
- ❏ Aluminum foil
- ❏ Biodegradable dish soap
- ❏ Water bottle to carry while hiking
- ❏ Water jug to fetch water from the pump or faucet
- ❏ Food and drinks (Remember that you'll have only as much capacity to keep things cold as you have cooler space. You and your children especially will be sure to work up hearty appetites being outdoors all day, so pack a good amount of food, including any condiments/spices you like while cooking. Fresh fruit and vegetables are always good options—they are quick and need no refrigeration—as are things like granola bars and trail mix.
- ❏ Hunting gear appropriate for the game you will be pursuing
- ❏ Dog food if you're bring a pet
- ❏ Dog leash

Campsite Index

Bald Eagle State Park, 88

Black Moshannon State Park, 86

Blue Knob State Park, 133

Buckaloons Recreation Area, 69

Caledonia State Park, 142

Chapman State Park, 72

Cherry Springs State Park, 99

Clear Creek State Park, 80

Codorus State Park, 153

Colonel Crawford Park, 39

Colonel Denning State Park, 145

Colton Point State Park, 96

Cook Forest State Park, 78

Cowanesque Lake Tompkins Campground, 102

Cowans Gap State Park, 141

Crooked Creek Lake, 43

Curwensville Lake, 86

Dewdrop Recreation Area, 65

Duman Lake County Park, 131

Elk State Park, 83

Fowlers Hollow State Park, 144

Frances Slocum State Park, 119

French Creek State Park, 156

Gifford Pinchot State Park, 153

Green Lane Park, 108

Greenwood Furnace State Park, 147

Handsome Lake Boat Access Campground, 63

Hearts Content Recreation Area, 70

Hibernia County Park, 108

Hickory Run State Park, 115

Hills Creek State Park, 101

Hooks Brook Boat Access Campground, 62

Hopewell Boat Access Campground, 63

Hyner Run State Park, 91

Kettle Creek State Park, 92

Keystone State Park, 46

Kiasutha Recreation Area, 67

Kooser State Park, 52

Lackawanna State Park, 120

Lake Towhee Park, 111

Lancaster County Central Park, 154

Larnard-Hornbrook County Park, 124

Laurel Hill State Park, 53

Leonard Harrison State Park, 95

Little Buffalo State Park, 146

Little Pine State Park, 91

Locust Lake State Park, 113

Loleta Recreation Area, 77

Loyalhanna Lake, 45

Lyman Run State Park, 98

Mahoning Creek– Lake Milton Loop Campground, 43

Mauch Chunk Lake Park, 114

Minister Creek Campground, 71

Morrison Boat Access Campground, 66

Ohiopyle State Park, 51

Ole Bull State Park, 94

Parker Dam State Park, 83

Patterson State Park, 99

Penn-Roosevelt State
Park, 146
Pine Grove Boat Access
Campground, 64
Pine Grove Furnace State
Park, 143
Poe Paddy State
Park, 150
Poe Valley State Park, 149
Prince Gallitzin State
Park, 132
Promised Land State
Park, 118
Pymatuning State
Park, 39
Raccoon Creek State
Park, 47
Ravensburg State
Park, 90
Raymond B. Winter State
Park, 151
Raystown Lake Nancy's
Campground, 138
Raystown Lake
Seven Points
Campground, 137
Raystown Lake
Susquehannock
Campground, 137

Red Bridge Recreation
Area, 68
Reeds Gap State
Park, 149
Ricketts Glen State
Park, 121
Ryerson Station State
Park, 48
Shawnee State Park, 140
Shenango River Lake, 41
Simon B. Elliott State
Park, 85
Sinnemahoning State
Park, 93
Sizerville State Park, 100
Sunfish Pond County
Park, 124
Tinicum Park, 112
Tioga–Hammond
Lakes Ives Run
Campground, 102
Tionesta Lake Glasner
Run Camping
Area, 76
Tionesta Lake Kellettville
Recreation Area, 77
Tionesta Lake Lackey
Flats Camping
Area, 76

Tionesta Lake Outflow
Recreation Area, 73
Tionesta Lake Recreation
Area, 74
Tobyhanna State
Park, 117
Tohickon Valley Park, 110
Tracy Ridge Recreation
Area, 82
Trough Creek State
Park, 135
Twin Lakes Recreation
Area, 81
Two Mile Run County
Park, 40
Willow Bay Recreation
Area, 61
Worlds End State
Park, 123
Youghiogheny River
Lake Outflow
Campground, 49
Youghiogheny River
Lake Yough Lake
Campground, 50

About the Author

Bob Frye is a longtime outdoor writer based near Harrisburg, Pennsylvania. He is the author of numerous other books, including *Best Hikes Near Pittsburgh, Best Easy Day Hikes: Pittsburgh, Paddling Pennsylvania,* and *Deer Wars: Science, Tradition and the Battle Over Managing Whitetails in Pennsylvania.* He lives in Cleona with his wife, Amanda.